THE BACON, BUTTER, BOURBON & CHOCOLATE COOKBOOK

Chef Bruno's

FAVOURITE INGREDIENTS

THE BACON, BUTTER, BOURBON & CHOCOLATE COOKBOOK

Chef Bruno's

FAVOURITE INGREDIENTS

BY CHEF

Bruno Feldeisen

PHOTOGRAPHY BY

Henry M Wu

whitecap

Whitecap Books

DESIGN Andrew Bagatella
EDITOR Patrick Geraghty
PROOFREADER Holly Doll
PHOTOGRAPHY BY Henry M Wu

Library and Archives Canada Cataloguing in Publication

Title: The bacon, butter, bourbon & chocolate cookbook : Chef Bruno's favourite ingredients / by Chef Bruno Feldeisen ; photography by Henry M. Wu.
Other titles: Bacon, butter, bourbon and chocolate cookbook
Names: Feldeisen, Bruno, author. | Wu, Henry M., photographer.
Description: Includes index.
Identifiers: Canadiana 20240376102 | ISBN 9781770503335 (softcover)
Subjects: LCSH: Cooking (Bacon) | LCSH: Cooking (Butter) | LCSH: Cooking (Bourbon whiskey) | LCSH: Cooking (Chocolate) | LCGFT: Cookbooks.
Classification: LCC TX714 .F455 2024 | DDC 641.5—dc23

Canada Council for the Arts
Conseil des arts du Canada

Whitecap Books acknowledges the financial support of the Government of Canada through the Canada Book Fund (CBF) for our publishing activities and the Province of British Columbia through the Book Publishing Tax Credit.

7 6 5 4 3 2 1

Printed in Canada by Copywell.

whitecap.ca

To my son Sergio,

A bundle of joy appeared in my life more than 12 years ago. I would walk around the maternity ward holding you in my arms, softly singing to your delicate ears the French song "A la clairefontaine". I was mesmerized by how beautiful and meaningful my life has become from the moment I first saw you. And today I am in awe of how beautiful and inspiring you have become.

I dedicate this book to you. Don't stop dreaming of snowy days on the hills; destroy as many skateboards as needed. Don't hold back and live a meaningful life, full of joy and happiness.

Your Dad

table of

CONTENTS

s'more in a jar
STYLISH ECLAIRS
Praline Bar
Warm Fruit Cobbler
cheesecake lollipops
BUTTERSCOTCH PUDDING
popcorn brûlée
Vietnamese Affogato
Frangipan Tart
CANELE
Melt my
Macaron tower
MADELEINE
Doughnut Showdown
S02E23
Religieuse
2014

PREFACE: THE POWER OF RECIPES

In Diversity We Find Strength

In my first cookbook, *Baking with Bruno,* I wrote about some of the ways immigrants have shaped food culture in their countries of adoption, highlighting European immigrants in particular. More than ever, it is important to recognize the contributions of immigrants from all corners of the globe, without whose influence the food we enjoy on our table wouldn't be possible: farmers, pickers, packers, drivers, cooks, bussers, waiters and storytellers; home cooks and bakers from boundless horizons that enrich our daily lives. Traditions from every part of the world enrich our daily meals.

Recipes are stories. They are tales that travel through time—gifts shared with us by witnesses of bygone eras, preserving memories of times spent with family and friends. They might be the only link to a past love, a scribbled piece of paper with only a few words and some numbers, holding so many powerful emotions.

The poetry of words and numbers contained in a recipe reminds future generations of their proud past. In the story told through cups, weights, volumes or sometimes just scribbled guesses, a recipe can take the reader on a remarkable journey. Cultures are built on recipes, and a recipe is one of the most precious items cooks carry with them on their journey to new horizons. It shapes the culinary future of a community, and acts as a powerful beacon of hope and identity. A world with no recipes is a world without an imagination.

Our planet is indeed a huge garden, and the presence of real and relevant food stories is always alive, no matter where those stories originate from. Food is life and food matters everywhere.

Bruno Feldeisen

THE WORLD'S No. 1 BOURBON WHISKEY
LE MEILLEUR BOURBON AU MONDE
JIM BEAM
JIM BEAM
B
SINCE 1795

INTRODUCTION

Bacon Butter Bourbon Chocolate

Four distinct ingredients and flavours. Each one remarkable on its own, and together they produce a range of tastes and experiences that we humans are greedy for: salty, sweet, silky, chewy. These four ingredients—from the old world to the new world—merge my past, present and future.

Butter is often a "support" ingredient, but its flavour and texture unarguably enhance any recipe it's found in. No other fat can carry the same range of flavours or emotions. So many important factors are involved in making a great butter: the ethical way the cattle are raised, their diet, the season in which they graze, the fat content. While France produces some of the world's best butters, you will find, while perusing your local farmers' market, that a lot of local dairy farms offer their own buttery products that are as good or, sometimes, even better than the international kind. I spread a generous amount of butter on my country bread before adding slices of artisanal cheese on top. Same with charcuterie—that's how I roll.

Bacon, with its hypnotizing aroma, has an irrational draw for even the most committed non-meat eater—and it's here in North America where you will find the most delicious bacon. This is where it's done right: crispy, deep-fried, chopped, in stews, dipped in chocolate. Bacon frying slowly in a cast iron pan early in the morning as the sun rises is the stuff of unforgettable sensory memories. That said, it is more important than ever to support an ethical food supply, and we should strive to affect positive change in the way hogs are raised and slaughtered. Animals raised humanely, without hormones, are the future, not to mention, cured and smoked meats from animals handled ethically simply taste better.

Bourbon, that quintessential American-made drink with its sweet vanilla tones and oakiness, possesses an enticing smoky flavour that can elevate a recipe. From classic cocktails to fruit stews and baked cakes, bourbon is one of the best liquors to use in baking and cooking. It adds a unique flavour that evokes an older time's sensibility and invites you to sit back and relax after a long day.

Chocolate is how my culinary career began, as an apprentice at a chocolatier in France. In the early hours of the day, when most people were still sound asleep, I would turn out huge containers of melted dark chocolate onto a cold white slab of marble as big as a king-size bed and, using arm-length spatulas, start the process of tempering the chocolate for that day's creations. Imagine a young man, barely 16 years old, elbow-deep in melted chocolate, manipulating a hundred pounds of melted chocolate across a marble expanse. Chocolate truly is a small taste of heaven on earth. I've heard a rumour that there are some who don't adore chocolate, but, if so, I believe them to be a mere few.

This collection of delicious recipes has some of my old favourites as well as new ones. So come with me on this delectable culinary adventure, have a tremendous amount of fun and, very importantly, do not forget to share your delicious bakes and creations with family, friends and colleagues.

BRUNO'S BAKING & COOKING TIPS

BAKING TEMPERATURE The baking times and temperatures noted in this book are just for reference—no two ovens bake quite the same, and you might need to adjust your oven temperature by a few degrees. An important point to remember is to avoid opening your oven door too frequently to check on your baking. Every time you open the door the temperature will drop, and closing the door will push cooler air inside. As a result, the baking will take longer, altering the moisture content, which tends to make your food dryer.

BAKING TIME A gas oven bakes differently from an electric oven, and there are even more differences when using an oven fan. All the recipes in this book have been tested using a basic electric stove with no fan.

BUTTER VS. SALTED BUTTER I only use unsalted butter and I adjust the saltiness of all my recipes using sea salt. On the rare occasion I do use salted butter, it is because the butter is crafted in an artisanal manner with real sea salt crystals.

MEASURING INGREDIENTS There are two options when measuring ingredients: volume or weight. Volume uses cups, teaspoons, etc., which is easy to use but not always accurate. For example, flours can have different densities based on the season and the quality of the flour. A cup of one brand of flour might be a bit heavier than another, which isn't a very big deal when using one or two cups in a recipe, but increased volumes create a huge discrepancy that could affect the recipe. Weight is accurate, so investing in a small electronic scale is a good tool to have in your kitchen. The drawback? Most cookbooks are written with volume measurements, not weight.

PREPARATION TIMES AND SET-UP There is no need to prepare all your baking the day you need it. Cookie doughs can be made a few days ahead and baked when you need them, freeing up much needed time for other preparations. A pie dough can be lined in a tart shell and frozen until needed.

FREEZER One of the great things about baking is that you can prepare a lot of recipes in advance and just store them in a freezer. Doughs can be prepared and divided into small portions and stored in a freezer—take out and bake only what you need. Proper planning takes away the stress of preparing everything the same day or at the last minute.

TOOLS OF THE TRADE

I could write pages on what equipment is needed to be a baker, and my kitchen is a testament to how much one baker can think they need to acquire. The truth is, you don't need a lot to be a successful baker and can start, over time, building your baking tool inventory. There are plenty of discount stores out there that sell kitchen and baking wares at reasonable prices. Here's my guide to helpful tools to have in your kitchen:

BLOWTORCH The best tool to caramelize the top of crème brûlée.

CANDY THERMOMETER Also called a sugar thermometer. I use a basic one.

CUTTERS It's good to have a set of both straight and fluted ones.

DEEP PANS You'll need at least one springform pan for baking cheesecakes or custards.

ELECTRIC MIXER Always the most expensive piece of equipment. You can do without for a while, but it is a challenge, especially when making cookies.

KNIVES There are plenty of great knives at reasonable prices, unless of course you aspire to be a sushi master. A small paring knife, bread knife and chef's knife will do.

MOULDS Cake moulds in different shapes and forms enhance presentations and visual appeal, although a creative baker can always use an empty soup can or metal object to craft something unique.

PASTRY BRUSH A brush with synthetic bristles will be easier to clean and sanitize.

PIPING BAGS Disposable plastic bags are more sanitary.

PIPING TIPS It's handy to have an assorted set with different sizes.

ICE CREAM SCOOP Useful if you need to portion and scoop cookies and muffins.

ROLLING PIN Always use a wooden rolling pin. I mostly use the French style, but it is easier to use a rolling pin with handles.

SAUCEPANS You'll need small, medium and large.

SCALE AND MEASURING TOOLS A digital scale, measuring spoons, a liquid measuring cup and a set of dry measuring cups are all important to ensure accuracy.

SHEET TRAYS Get shallow rectangular sheet trays with a 1-inch (2.5 cm) lip on all four sides. Be sure they fit in your oven, fridge and freezer before buying them.

SMALL SIEVE This will let you strain all your custards, curds and sauces.

SPATULA For different occasions, invest in small, medium and large spatulas, both straight and offset.

WHISK Medium-size whisks, both rigid and balloon style, are great for creating aeration in a foam.

WOODEN SPOON Get a medium-size spoon to stir jams and fruit sauces as they cook.

ZESTER The Microplane brand is the best.

MY PANTRY

It is no secret that a recipe is only as delicious as the quality of the ingredients we put in it. And what better way to spend a weekend morning than searching through farmers' markets for that fully ripened seasonal fruit that will make your fruit pie the rock star of any party. Quality ingredients are authentic, seasonal and ethical, and truly reflect the local terroir. Together, quality ingredients are the cornerstone of great baking or cooking.

Below are some notes on what to store in your pantry to be a happy cook and baker.

FLOUR Cake flour has the lowest amount of gluten protein, which helps any batter to "crumble" once baked. It's perfect for cookies and sponges. Pastry flour has more gluten protein and works well as cake batter. All-purpose flour is great for some cookie doughs and pizza. Bread flour has the most gluten protein and is typically used in breadmaking.

GINGER Candied Australian ginger is a must. Soft, floral and not overly sweet, it carries the right kick to enhance your recipes. I prefer to use finely chopped candied ginger in any recipe rather than ginger powder, even holiday cookies.

HONEY Read the label carefully. Lots of honeys are a blend from different countries with an added sweetener like corn syrup. There is no reason to buy imported honey when locally produced honey is often available in locally owned food stores and farmers' markets.

MAPLE SYRUP Be sure to use 100% pure maple syrup. It's a bit pricey, but better that any "flavoured maple syrup" laced with corn syrup.

NUTS I stock whole, sliced and ground nuts: pecans, walnuts, almonds and hazelnuts. Keep them in airtight containers in your freezer to keep them fresh. Pine nuts are a good, cheap alternative when other nuts can be too pricey. I find you can often switch nuts in recipes without making too many adjustments.

EXTRA VIRGIN OLIVE OIL I like my olive oil fruity, slightly peppery and a beautiful vibrant green colour. And good olive oil does not need to be expensive. The bottle I buy is usually in the 10 to 14 dollar range for 3 cups (750 mL).

SALT Salt is important in recipes both as a flavour-enhancer and a preservative. I use sea salt in all my recipes, except when I sear or grill meat; on those occasions I use kosher salt. Sea salt is made from the natural evaporation of sea water and is mined in large deposits. It comes in different grain sizes and colours. All sea salts have a wonderful natural aroma that does a beautiful job binding all the flavours in a recipe. And, contrary to popular culture, a good sea salt is not expensive.

SPICES I recommend cinnamon, nutmeg, turmeric, coriander and cardamom, either ground or in their natural form.

SUGAR Granulated, light brown and icing sugar are the three main sugars needed. Every sugar adds its own distinct feature in a recipe. A key point to remember is that white sugar is not vegan. In most cases, cane juice is passed through filters filled with crushed beef bones to remove impurities from the sugar syrup.

VANILLA It's good to stock both vanilla beans and 100% pure vanilla extract. Read the label when buying vanilla extract and stay away from artificial flavouring like vanillin—a synthetic chemical extracted from wood products.

– chapter 1 –

BACON

BACON

CURED SALTED PORK belly means bacon for breakfast, bacon for lunch, bacon for dinner, bacon for snacking, bacon forever.

To pick the right bacon, you want to find one with the right amount of fat to meat. Also, the way it is cured, smoked or flavoured is important. Choosing a more artisanal crafted bacon will, of course, bring unique and authentic flavours that can play beautifully in any dish.

Always save the bacon fat from the cooking process. It can be reused to cook other dishes.

CRISPY BACON AND BACON BITS

{ MAKES 1 CUP (250 ML) CHOPPED BACON BITS }

Good, tasty bacon is all about the tight balance of flavours created by the curing, the quality of the meat and how the smoking is done. Picking the right product is important. If you're chopping your bacon into bits, fresh is always so much better than packaged, which is often overly salty and of poor quality.

INSTRUCTIONS Preheat oven to 350°F (175°C).

In a large sauté pan, heat the canola oil over medium heat. Add the bacon slices and fry until crispy. Remove sauté pan from heat and, using a pair of cooking tongs, place the fried bacon on a paper towel–lined baking tray to allow the fat to drain.

BACON BITS: Once cooled, place bacon strips on a cutting board and chop into small pieces using a large chef's knife. Place the chopped bacon bits on a parchment-lined baking tray and place in oven for 5 minutes to dry.

Remove from the oven and allow to cool. Place in an airtight container until needed.

INGREDIENTS

1 Tbsp (15 mL) canola oil

10 bacon strips

BACON AND SALMON ROE DEVILED EGGS

{ MAKES 6 DEVILED EGGS }

This surf and turf version of deviled eggs is a fun and tasty bite that's perfect for a cocktail party nibble or pre-dinner appetizer. The addition of delicate salmon roe blends sublimely with the rich earthiness of crispy bacon.

INGREDIENTS

3 large eggs

1 Tbsp (15 mL) baking soda, for the boiling water

¼ cup (60 mL) mayonnaise

1 Tbsp (15 mL) Dijon mustard

1 Tbsp (15 mL) extra virgin olive oil

1 tsp (5 mL) Worcestershire sauce

3 fully cooked and crispy bacon strips (see page 13)

½ cup (125 mL) salmon roe

1 Tbsp (15 mL) chopped chives for serving

INSTRUCTIONS In a medium saucepan, place the eggs and cover with cold water. Add baking soda to the water (it will make it easier to peel the cooked eggs). Place the saucepan over medium heat and bring to a boil; remove from heat and let the eggs rest in the hot water for 12 minutes.

Remove eggs from the pot and place in a small bowl with ice cold water for 30 minutes, then remove eggs from the water and refrigerate for 4 hours.

Peel and cut the cooked eggs in half lengthwise. Remove yolks and place in a small bowl with the mayonnaise, Dijon mustard, olive oil and Worcestershire sauce. Using a small hand whisk, stir until smooth, then spoon the yolk filling equally among the 6 egg-white halves.

Break the bacon strips into 12 uneven pieces. Top each egg with 2 pieces of bacon and a spoonful of salmon roe and sprinkle with chopped chives. Serve on a platter.

BACON AND ROASTED GARLIC POLENTA PIE

{ MAKES 8 SERVINGS }

Old school, but a really delicious treat. This savoury pie is good on its own, served as a side dish with barbecued meats or featured on a buffet platter. It can be served straight from the cast iron pan, rustic and yummy.

INGREDIENTS

1 cup (250 mL) unsalted butter

½ cup (125 mL) extra virgin olive oil

½ yellow onion, peeled and finely diced

1 tsp (5 mL) chopped thyme

4 large garlic cloves, peeled

2 cups (500 mL) whole milk

½ cup (125 mL) water

1 cup (250 mL) cornmeal, finely ground

½ tsp (2.5 mL) sea salt

1 cup (250 mL) Parmesan cheese, grated

½ cup (125 mL) sour cream

1 cup (250 mL) crispy bacon bits (see page 13)

1 tsp (5 mL) cayenne pepper

INSTRUCTIONS In a medium saucepan, melt the butter over medium heat. Add the olive oil, onion, thyme and garlic and cook slowly, stirring with a wooden spoon, until the mixture becomes light golden in colour (about 5 minutes). Add the milk, water, cornmeal and salt and continue cooking over low heat until the mixture starts to thicken, about 10 minutes.

Remove saucepan from heat and add the Parmesan, sour cream, bacon bits and cayenne pepper. Pour the batter into an 8-inch (20 cm) parchment-lined cast iron pan and refrigerate for 3 hours.

Heat oven to 360°F (180°C), then place the cooled mixture in the oven and bake for 15 minutes, or until the top is light golden in colour. Remove from the oven and let it rest for 10 minutes.

Cut the pie into 8 portions and serve.

WARM BACON, SMOKED OYSTER AND CHIVE SCONES

{ MAKES 12 SCONES }

This is one of the most unusual recipes I have ever crafted for a seafood menu, and the result was uniquely delicious. The richness of the smoked oysters elevates the buttery flavour of the scones, with a hint of saltiness from the bacon. Note that the recipe has no added salt because the bacon contributes plenty. The scones perfectly complement a seafood dish like a cioppino, smoked salmon or any grilled fish.

INGREDIENTS

1½ cups (375 mL) all-purpose flour

¼ cup (60 mL) granulated sugar

2 Tbsp (30 mL) chopped chives

¼ cup (60 mL) crispy bacon bits (see page 13)

1 tsp (5 mL) baking powder

½ tsp (2.5 mL) baking soda

½ cup (125 mL) diced cold unsalted butter

One 2 oz (60 g) can smoked oysters

1 cup (250 mL) buttermilk

INSTRUCTIONS Preheat oven to 360°F (180°C).

Using an electric mixing bowl with the paddle attachment, combine the flour, sugar, chives, bacon bits, baking powder and baking soda on low speed. Add the diced butter and smoked oysters, including their marinating oil, and mix on low speed until the butter and smoked oysters almost blend into the flour mix. Add the buttermilk and mix just enough for the dough to start to come together.

Using a soup spoon, shape 12 scones and drop them onto a parchment-lined baking sheet, spacing them about 2 inches (5 cm) apart from each other. Bake for 30 minutes or until the tops of the scones are light golden coloured. Remove from the oven and place scones on a wire rack.

Scones are best served warm or reheated.

BACON CHEDDAR SCONES

{ MAKES 6 SCONES }

These scones are warm pillows packed with flavour. Perfectly complementing a hearty soup or simple omelette, these fluffy, buttery scones are easy and fast to make.

INSTRUCTIONS Preheat oven to 360°F (180°C).

In a medium bowl, whisk together all the dry ingredients. Cut in the butter with a pastry blender or two knives until incorporated as pea-size pieces. With a fork, stir in the grated cheese, then add the bacon bits and stir until evenly distributed in the flour mixture.

In a small bowl, beat the egg into the cream, then add to the dry ingredients and mix with the fork. Add the milk and mix until all the dry ingredients are fully incorporated. If it seems a bit dry, add an extra 1 Tbsp (15 mL) whole milk as needed, but you don't want the dough to be wet.

Turn the dough out onto a lightly floured work surface. Knead lightly with your hands for a few seconds to ensure all the dry bits are worked into the dough, then flatten the dough into a disc or rectangle (depending on your cutter shape) with a thickness of ¾ inch (2 cm). Cut out 6 scone shapes and place on a parchment-lined baking sheet. Brush the tops of the scones with cream.

Bake for 14 to 17 minutes, until the tops are toasty golden brown in colour. Check the scones' progress at 12 minutes; you don't want them overdone. Remove from the oven and cool on a rack.

INGREDIENTS

2 cups (500 mL) all-purpose flour

2 tsp (10 mL) baking powder

1 tsp (5 mL) baking soda

½ tsp (2.5 mL) sea salt

1 Tbsp (15 mL) granulated sugar

½ cup (125 mL) cold unsalted butter

1 cup (250 mL) grated sharp cheddar cheese

1 cup (250 mL) crispy bacon bits (see page 13)

1 large egg

½ cup (125 mL) heavy cream + 2 Tbsp (30 mL) for brushing the tops of the scones

¼ cup (60 mL) whole milk + more as needed

BACON AND GOAT CHEESE CUSTARD POTS

{ MAKES 6 CUSTARDS }

This is a great custard for two reasons: it's simple to make, and it's highly addictive. Savoury, creamy and a bit smoky, it's delicious served warm—perfect for a buffet dinner or as a first course.

INGREDIENTS

1 cup (250 mL) whipping cream

1 cup (250 mL) whole milk

2 large eggs

3 egg yolks

½ tsp (2.5 mL) sea salt

¼ tsp (1 mL) cayenne pepper

½ cup (125 mL) crispy bacon bits (see page 13)

2 Tbsp (30 mL) chopped fresh chives

½ cup (125 mL) crumbled goat cheese

2 Tbsp (30 mL) extra virgin olive oil

¼ tsp (1 mL) fresh ground black pepper

INSTRUCTIONS Preheat oven to 340°F (170°C).

In a medium saucepan, heat the whipping cream and milk over medium heat until simmering. Set aside until needed.

In a medium bowl, whisk together the eggs and yolks using a hand whisk. Add the sea salt, cayenne pepper, bacon bits and chives. Stir in the warm cream and milk.

Sprinkle equal amounts of crumbled goat cheese into 6 ramequins. Ladle an equal amount of the egg mixture into each ramequin, stirring before each pour to ensure each ramequin gets an equal amount of bacon and chives.

Place the ramequins into a deep dish pan. Pour 3 cups (750 mL) warm water into the pan to create a bath for the ramequins to sit in. Place pan on the bottom rack of the oven and bake for 30 minutes or until the centre of each custard starts to set. Remove from the oven and place ramekins on a cooking rack.

Custards are best served lukewarm.

HOMEMADE BACON MAYO

{ MAKES 1 CUP (250 ML) MAYONNAISE }

After tasting homemade mayonnaise, it might be a challenge to go back to the commercially produced kind. The preparation is a bit technical, which can be frustrating if the final result is a loose "broken" texture, but once mastered this is a great condiment to add to your table. This delicious recipe will enhance your sandwiches and tuna or egg salads, and it will simply give you something to dunk your fried chicken morsels into. Adding bacon to homemade mayonnaise makes it a special treat.

INGREDIENTS

¾ cup (180 mL) canola oil

¼ cup (60 mL) extra virgin olive oil

3 egg yolks

3 tsp (15 mL) apple cider vinegar

¼ cup (60 mL) crispy bacon bits (see page 13), with bacon fat from the tray

INSTRUCTIONS Pour both oils into a single container you can pour from.

Place the egg yolks and apple cider vinegar in a food processor. Mix on high speed while slowly pouring in the oils—do not pour the oil too quickly or the mayonnaise will split and have an oily look. Add the cold bacon fat from the pan.

Once the mayonnaise is mixed into a smooth texture, transfer it to a storage container. Stir in the cold chopped bacon bits and refrigerate up to 10 days.

BACON PARMESAN THYME SHORTBREAD

{ MAKES 60 SHORTBREAD PIECES }

I am passionate about making shortbread—they are the perfect recipe to play with flavours. If you maintain the same ratio of dry ingredients to butter you can just play with different herbs and spices. This particular shortbread is buttery with a hint of thyme, and delivers a spectacular punch of bacon and cheese flavours. Delicious on its own, it perfectly pairs with a cheese or charcuterie plate.

INGREDIENTS

2 Tbsp (30 mL) extra virgin olive oil

1½ cups (375 mL) granulated sugar

½ tsp (2.5 mL) sea salt

2 tsp (10 mL) pure vanilla extract

2¼ cups (560 mL) softened unsalted butter

1 large egg + 2 large eggs for egg wash

4 cups (1 L) cake flour

2 tsp (10 mL) fresh chopped thyme

¾ cup (180 mL) shredded Parmesan cheese

1½ cups (375 mL) crispy bacon bits (see page 13)

1 tsp (5 mL) fresh grated lemon zest

INSTRUCTIONS Preheat oven to 370°F (185°C).

In an electric mixing bowl with the paddle attachment, cream together the sugar, sea salt, vanilla extract and butter on low speed. Scrape down the sides of the bowl from time to time to ensure the butter mixture is well combined and free of lumps. Add 1 egg.

In a separate medium bowl, stir together the cake flour, thyme, Parmesan, bacon bits and lemon zest, then add it to the butter mixture. Mix slowly on low speed until the dough comes together. Avoid overmixing.

Spread the mixture over the entire surface of a parchment-lined baking sheet and use a rolling pin to make sure the dough covers the entire surface. Using a fork, poke holes into the entire surface of the dough. Beat the remaining eggs in a small bowl with a fork and brush the egg wash over the entire surface of the shortbread.

Place the pan on the middle rack of the oven and bake for about 35 minutes, or until the top is a light golden-brown colour. Remove from the oven to a cooling rack.

While still warm, use a paring knife and metal ruler to cut the shortbread into 3 × 1–inch (7 × 2.5 cm) rectangles. Let the baking sheet cool completely, then lift each piece from the tray using a small offset spatula. Place in an airtight container and store in a cool dry place. Shortbread are good stored this way for up to 1 month.

POMPE AUX GRATTONS

{ MAKES 8 SERVINGS }

I spent my teenage years in a small town in the centre of France called Moulins-sur-Allier. It is in the Bourbonnais area, south of Burgundy—an area that always reminded me of Tuscany. The pompe aux grattons, a round loaf, is a Bourbonnais specialty served lukewarm during aperitif hours that pairs perfectly with a glass of red wine. It is sold in most local bakeries and has a very rustic look similar to a brioche dough.

INSTRUCTIONS Dissolve the instant yeast in the warm water.

In an electric mixing bowl with the hook attachment, mix the flour, sea salt and cold butter on low speed for about 5 minutes. Add the 3 eggs, dissolved yeast and Worcestershire sauce. Mix until the dough comes together in a ball around the hook. Add the bacon bits and mix just enough for them to be incorporated.

Remove the hook and let the dough rest in the bowl, covering the top with a clean kitchen towel. Let it sit at room temperature for 2 hours.

Preheat oven to 340°F (170°C).

Turn the dough out onto a lightly floured work surface and shape into a circle about 9 inches (23 cm) in diameter. Place the dough on a parchment-lined baking tray. Beat the remaining egg in a small bowl and brush the egg wash over the top of the dough. Sprinkle with the large flake salt.

Bake for 40 minutes or until the dough is a golden colour. Remove from the oven and let cool on a wire rack. Best served slightly warm.

INGREDIENTS

1 tsp (5 mL) instant yeast

1 tsp (5 mL) warm water

2 cups (500 mL) bread flour

½ tsp (2.5 mL) sea salt

1 cup (250 mL) diced cold unsalted butter

3 large eggs + 1 large egg for egg wash

2 Tbsp (30 mL) Worcestershire sauce

½ cup (125 mL) crispy bacon bits (see page 13)

1 Tbsp (15 mL) large flake salt

GRILLED ASPARAGUS WITH APPLE CIDER BACON VINAIGRETTE

{ MAKES 4 SERVINGS }

Grilled asparagus is simple to make and lets you enjoy a tasty, flavourful and healthy dish. It is quick to make on a grill, taking only minutes, and will make an impression at any barbecue when served with this delicious vinaigrette. It's a perfect summer treat.

GRILLED ASPARAGUS

1 bunch green asparagus

2 Tbsp (30 mL) extra virgin olive oil

Salt and pepper to taste

APPLE CIDER BACON VINAIGRETTE

3 Tbsp (45 mL) Dijon mustard

1 Tbsp (15 mL) honey

¼ cup (60 mL) extra virgin olive oil

¼ cup (60 mL) apple juice

¼ cup (60 mL) apple cider vinegar

¼ cup (60 mL) crispy bacon bits (see page 13)

Salt and pepper to taste

INSTRUCTIONS FOR GRILLED ASPARAGUS Light your barbecue and set it to medium heat.

Trim about 20 percent off the base of the asparagus. In a medium bowl, add the asparagus and toss with olive oil, salt and pepper.

Using tongs, place asparagus side-by-side on the grill and cook until the tips start to char. Remove from the grill and place on a parchment-lined baking tray.

INSTRUCTIONS FOR APPLE CIDER BACON VINAIGRETTE In a small bowl, whisk together the Dijon mustard, honey and olive oil. Add the apple juice, apple cider vinegar and bacon bits and season with salt and pepper as needed.

ASSEMBLY Drizzle the grilled asparagus with vinaigrette right before serving.

BACON AND STILTON CHEESE MASHED POTATOES

{ MAKES 4 SERVINGS }

Perfect mashed potatoes require the right potato. For me, Yukon Gold is the ideal choice—it is good baked, roasted or cut into fries, and as mash potatoes it is the gold standard. This dish is my go-to comfort food. Whether on its own, drizzled with melted butter or gravy or as a side dish, it is happiness for your tummy and soul.

INSTRUCTIONS Place the diced potatoes and whole garlic cloves in a large pot of salted water. Place over high heat, bring to a boil and cook for about 20 minutes, until the potatoes and garlic are soft.

Drain the water through a fine mesh strainer and return potatoes and garlic to the pot. Mash the potatoes and garlic until smooth, then add the whipping cream and melted butter. Place the pot back on the stove over low heat and stir with a wooden spoon until the cream is incorporated. Add salt and pepper to taste.

Remove pot from heat. Incorporate the olive oil, sour cream and bacon bits. Gently add the crumbled Stilton cheese.

Pour the mixture into 4 ramequins and sprinkle the tops of the potatoes with chopped chives. Serve while still hot.

INGREDIENTS

3 cups (750 mL) peeled and diced Yukon Gold potatoes

6 garlic cloves, peeled

1 cup (250 mL) whipping cream

½ cup (125 mL) melted unsalted butter

Salt and pepper to taste

½ cup (125 mL) extra virgin olive oil

½ cup (125 mL) sour cream

½ cup (125 mL) crispy bacon bits (see page 13)

½ cup (125 mL) crumbled Stilton cheese

2 Tbsp (30 mL) chopped chives for serving

BACON, OYSTER AND CORN CHOWDER

{ MAKES 4 SERVINGS }

Every port city in North America has its own version of a chowder. I do like a classic chowder with salmon, but nothing beats the briny flavour of this version. The key is not to cook the oysters on the stove but instead let the heat of the chowder slowly and gently warm them and capture their delicate flavours. The results are rich and satisfying.

INGREDIENTS

2 Tbsp (30 mL) unsalted butter

¼ cup (60 mL) extra virgin olive oil

½ cup (125 mL) diced celery

½ cup (125 mL) diced onion

½ cup (125 mL) diced carrot

1 cup (250 mL) diced peeled potatoes

1 tsp (5 mL) dry thyme

1 Tbsp (15 mL) chopped garlic

1 cup (250 mL) clam juice

Salt and pepper to taste

⅓ cup (80 mL) all-purpose flour

2 cups (500 mL) whole milk

1 cup (250 mL) whipping cream

1 cup (250 mL) frozen corn

1 cup (250 mL) fresh shucked oysters

½ cup (125 mL) crispy bacon bits (see page 13), divided

1 Tbsp (15 mL) chopped chives for serving

INSTRUCTIONS In a large pot, melt the butter over medium heat. Add the olive oil, celery, onion and carrot and sauté for about 5 minutes, stirring with a wooden spoon. Add the diced potatoes, thyme and garlic and sauté for another 5 minutes until all ingredients are slightly cooked.

Add the clam juice and salt and pepper to taste and bring to a boil. Whisk the flour into the milk and stir into the pot. Simmer over low heat for 10 minutes.

Add the whipping cream and corn. Cook for another 5 minutes.

Remove pot from the stove and stir in the fresh oysters and ¼ cup (60 mL) chopped bacon. Pour the soup into bowls and garnish with the remaining bacon bits and chopped chives. Serve while hot.

BACON AND GOAT CHEESE RISOTTO

{ MAKES 4 SERVINGS }

The key to a great risotto is to cook it slowly and let the rice slowly absorb the olive oil, followed by the white wine, then the chicken stock. It is important to use a wide saucepan so that you can easily stir the rice using a wooden spoon. I do not use butter or cream in any of my risotto recipes, I just let the starch from the rice create the creamy texture.

INSTRUCTIONS In a sauté pan, warm 2 Tbsp (30 mL) olive oil over medium heat and add the shallots and onions; add the garlic and cook until the mixture is translucent. Add the arborio rice while stirring with a wooden spoon. Add the white wine and keep stirring until the wine is absorbed by the rice. Add the thyme and rosemary. Slowly add the chicken stock and stir continuously until absorbed by the rice. The texture should be creamy.

Once the rice is al dente, remove pan from the stove and stir in the Parmesan. Add salt and pepper to taste. Stir in the goat cheese, bacon bits and remaining olive oil right before serving.

INGREDIENTS

¼ cup (60 mL) extra virgin olive oil, divided

½ tsp (2.5 mL) chopped shallots

½ cup (125 mL) diced onions

½ tsp (2.5 mL) chopped garlic

1½ cups (325 mL) arborio rice

¼ cup (60 mL) white wine

¼ tsp (1 mL) chopped thyme

¼ tsp (1 mL) chopped rosemary

4 cups (1 L) low sodium chicken stock

½ cup (125 mL) grated Parmesan

Salt and pepper to taste

¾ cup (180 mL) crumbled goat cheese

½ cup (125 mL) crispy bacon bits (see page 13)

BACON AND CASHEW BRITTLE

{ MAKES 36 PIECES }

Crunchy, chewy and salty, this brittle recipe is a perfect mashup of texture and sweet and savoury flavours. It's the perfect snack to enjoy with red wine, or you can chop the brittle into smaller pieces to sprinkle on top of vanilla, coffee or chocolate ice cream.

INGREDIENTS

¼ cup (60 mL) whipping cream

¼ cup (60 mL) water

¼ cup (60 mL) honey

1 tsp (5 mL) vanilla extract

1 cup (250 mL) granulated sugar

¼ cup (60 mL) light brown sugar

½ cup (125 mL) softened unsalted butter

½ cup (125 mL) crispy bacon bits (see page 13)

1 cup (250 mL) chopped cashews

¼ cup (60 mL) toasted sesame seeds

1 tsp (5 mL) baking soda

¼ tsp (1 mL) ground cinnamon

INSTRUCTIONS In a medium saucepan, combine the whipping cream, water, honey, vanilla and both sugars. Cook over medium heat, stirring occasionally, until the mixture reaches a temperature of 255°F (125°C). Remove from heat and whisk in the butter.

Return pan to the stove and bring the mixture to a boil while continuously stirring until the mixture reaches 290°F (145°C). Remove from heat and stir in the bacon, cashews, sesame seeds and baking soda. Let it sit for 2 minutes until no longer foaming.

Spread the mixture onto a parchment-lined baking tray in a thin layer and place on a cooling rack. Once cooled, snap brittle into 1½-inch (4 cm) triangles and store in an airtight container in a cool place up to 1 month.

BACON CHURROS WITH BACON CHOCOLATE SAUCE

{ MAKES 24 CHURROS }

In my life, I have been lucky enough to live in two different places that make wonderful churros: the Basque country in Spain and France, and Los Angeles, California. I just loved walking around downtown LA and grabbing those gigantic pinwheeled churros off a cart. I add bacon in this concoction for a delicious combination of saltiness and cinnamon. It's difficult to resist dipping my fingers in the chocolate sauce to finish off any remaining bits.

BACON CHURROS

½ cup (125 mL) water

½ cup (125 mL) whole milk

⅔ cup (160 mL) granulated sugar, divided

1 tsp (5 mL) sea salt

6 Tbsp (90 mL) unsalted butter

1 cup (250 mL) all-purpose flour

2 large eggs

1 tsp (5 mL) pure vanilla extract

½ cup (125 mL) crispy bacon bits (see page 13)

1 Tbsp (15 mL) ground cinnamon

CHOCOLATE SAUCE

¼ cup (60 mL) whole milk

¾ cup (180 mL) whipping cream

¼ cup (60 mL) granulated sugar

3 Tbsp (45 mL) honey

1 tsp (5 mL) vanilla extract

¼ tsp (1 mL) sea salt

¾ cup (180 mL) chopped extra bitter chocolate

¼ cup (60 mL) crispy bacon bits (see page 13), with bacon fat from the tray

INSTRUCTIONS FOR BACON CHURROS In a medium saucepan, combine the water, milk, 2 Tbsp (30 mL) sugar, sea salt and butter and bring to a boil. Using a wooden spatula, stir in the flour and cook over medium heat until the dough comes away from the sides of the saucepan, about 2 minutes.

Transfer the dough to an electric mixing bowl with the whisk attachment and mix on medium speed. In a small bowl, whisk the 2 eggs and add to mixing bowl. Keep mixing at medium speed for about 2 minutes, stopping midway to scrape down the sides of the bowl with a rubber spatula. Add the vanilla extract and bacon bits and mix for another 30 seconds.

Remove the still-warm dough from the bowl and spoon into a star-tipped piping bag. Pipe finger-width strips about 4 inches (10 cm) in length onto a parchment-lined baking tray. Place the tray in the freezer for 1 hour to firm up the piped dough.

In a medium-deep saucepan, warm 3¾ cups (935 mL) canola oil to 365°F (185°C). Gently place the frozen piped churros into the hot oil, using tongs to flip them. When they turn a light golden colour, remove them from the pan and place on a paper towel–lined tray for about a minute to drain off any oil.

Mix together the remaining granulated sugar and ground cinnamon and spread it out on a parchment-lined baking tray. While still warm, roll the churros in the cinnamon sugar.

INSTRUCTIONS FOR CHOCOLATE SAUCE In a small saucepan, bring the milk, whipping cream, sugar, honey, vanilla extract and sea salt to a boil. Whisk in the chopped chocolate until smooth. Add the chopped bacon and bacon fat. Mix until fully incorporated.

Serve chocolate sauce warm alongside the crispy and warm churros for dipping.

SPICY CANDIED CHOCOLATE BACON

{ MAKES 12 STRIPS }

I eat these evil (as in, I can't resist temptation) candied bacon strips for breakfast. Then, I have more for lunch. And inevitably, a few more for dinner. And that's the way I make my day a happy one.

INGREDIENTS

12 slices uncooked bacon

¼ cup (60 mL) maple syrup

½ cup (125 mL) light brown sugar

2 tsp (10 mL) cayenne pepper

2 tsp (10 mL) finely chopped fresh thyme

1 tsp (5 mL) ground cinnamon

¾ cup (180 mL) chopped bittersweet chocolate

INSTRUCTIONS Preheat oven to 330°F (160°C).

Place the bacon slices in a small bowl and pour the maple syrup over them. Delicately stir with your hand until each slice is coated in maple syrup, then remove the slices one by one onto a parchment-lined baking tray. Sprinkle each slice with brown sugar, cayenne pepper, fresh thyme and cinnamon and bake for about 20 minutes. The bacon should be golden in colour and crispy. Cook longer if necessary.

Once cooked, remove each bacon slice using a pair of tongs and place on an oiled cooling rack (to avoid the candied bacon sticking to it). Once cooled, the bacon will be crispy.

Place a double boiler over medium heat. Add the bittersweet chocolate to the bowl, and allow it to melt slowly.

Using a fork, drizzle each candied bacon slice with some chocolate to create a zebra pattern.

PEANUT BUTTER, COFFEE AND BACON COOKIES

{ MAKES 12 COOKIES }

The saltiness found in these amazing cookies—a combination of bacon and peanut butter with a hint of coffee—is matched only by the salty tears of joy you'll cry after your first bite. This lip-smacking, chewy cookie is a bundle of sweet and salty perfection.

INSTRUCTIONS Preheat oven to 360°F (180°C).

In a medium bowl, stir together the flour, baking soda and baking powder.

In an electric mixing bowl with the paddle attachment, cream together the butter and light brown sugar on low speed. Scrape down the sides of the bowl using a rubber spatula to ensure a smooth dough. Mix for about 2 minutes, then add the egg and egg yolk and continue to mix until fully incorporated. The dough should be light and fluffy.

Add the flour mixture and combine on low speed until fully incorporated. Use the rubber spatula to scrape down the sides of the bowl as necessary. Add the bacon bits, chopped chocolate, creamy peanut butter and instant coffee, still mixing on low speed.

Using an ice cream scoop, form 12 dough balls and place them on a parchment-lined baking tray, spacing them 2 inches (5 cm) apart from each other. Flatten each cookie using wet fingers (so that the dough doesn't stick to your fingers). Using a small sieve, dust each flattened cookie with icing sugar.

Place the tray in the oven on the middle rack and bake for 13 minutes, until cookies are golden on their edges and still soft in their middles. Remove tray from oven and place on a cooling rack.

Store cooled cookies in an airtight container up to 1 month.

INGREDIENTS

1½ cups (375 mL) all-purpose flour

¼ tsp (1 mL) baking soda

¼ tsp (1 mL) baking powder

5 Tbsp (75 mL) unsalted butter

1 cup (250 mL) light brown sugar

1 large egg

1 egg yolk

½ cup (125 mL) crispy bacon bits (see page 13)

½ cup (125 mL) chopped milk chocolate

½ cup (125 mL) creamy peanut butter

1½ Tbsp (22.5 mL) instant coffee

¼ cup (60 mL) icing sugar

BACON COFFEE MARSHMALLOWS

{ MAKES 24 MARSHMALLOWS }

Making homemade marshmallows is a bit of a mashup of chemistry class and kitchen magic. There is a form of captivating wizardry in creating these cloudy and tasty little morsels of happiness.

INGREDIENTS

4 tsp (20 mL) unflavoured powdered gelatin

½ cup (125 mL) cold water

½ cup (125 mL) granulated sugar

¼ cup (60 mL) water

¼ cup (60 mL) maple syrup

½ cup (125 mL) light corn syrup

¼ tsp (1 mL) ground cardamom

¼ tsp (1 mL) instant coffee

½ cup (125 mL) crispy bacon bits (see page 13)

1 cup (250 mL) icing sugar

½ cup (125 mL) cornstarch

INSTRUCTIONS In a small bowl, dissolve the gelatin in ½ cup (125 mL) cold water and let it sit for 5 minutes until the gelatin blooms.

Line a baking tray with parchment paper and spray the entire surface with cooking oil.

In a medium saucepan, stir together the granulated sugar, ¼ cup (60 mL) water, maple syrup and corn syrup. Bring to a boil over medium heat, stirring occasionally. Check the temperature with a candy thermometer and cook until the mixture reaches 235°F (110°C).

Remove saucepan from heat and let it rest for 1 minute. Whisk the bloomed gelatin into the sugar mixture then immediately pour into an electric mixing bowl with the whisk attachment; whisk on medium speed for 5 minutes. Increase speed to high and whisk until the mixture starts to foam into a light and fluffy marshmallow texture.

Reduce speed to low and quickly incorporate the ground cardamom, instant coffee and bacon bits. Mix for 10 seconds only. While the fluffy marshmallow is still warm, spread it evenly over the prepared baking tray.

In a small bowl, stir together the icing sugar and cornstarch. Reserve a quarter of the sugar and cornstarch mixture for a later step; spoon the rest into a small sieve and dust over the entire surface of the marshmallow. Let the tray sit in a cool dry space for 3 hours.

Using a pair of scissors, cut the marshmallow into 1-inch (2.5 cm) squares and toss in the reserved sugar and cornstarch mixture until coated on all sides.

Place marshmallows in an airtight container and store in a dry and cool place. Over time, the marshmallows will start to dry up and lose their fluffiness, so it makes sense to eat them as quickly as possible.

WHOLE WHEAT BACON DOGGY BONE

{ MAKES 24 DOG TREATS }

Your human family members, friends and co-workers should not be the only ones enjoying your baking skills. Make your dog happy with these irresistible pet treats. Note: Not intended for human consumption!

INSTRUCTIONS Preheat oven to 370°F (185°C).

In a large bowl, stir together whole wheat flour, cornmeal and bread flour.

In a medium bowl, combine the chicken stock and milk.

Scrape the bacon fat from the baking tray and stir it into the flour mixture. Add the bacon bits, egg yolks and melted butter, then add the milk and chicken stock mixture to the flour mixture and blend with a wooden spatula, mixing until all ingredients are fully incorporated.

Turn the dough out onto a floured work surface and roll it to 1½ inches (4 cm) thick. Cut the dough into bone shapes using a cookie cutter (if you don't have a bone-shaped cutter, your dog will likely appreciate whichever shape you choose) and space them out on a parchment-lined baking tray about 2 inches (5 cm) apart from each other. Keep rolling the dough scraps to cut out more bone-shaped biscuits until all the dough is used up.

Bake for 15 minutes until the edges of the biscuits are light golden in colour, then transfer to a cooling rack.

Once cool, store dog treats in an airtight container at room temperature for up to 10 days.

INGREDIENTS

2 cups (500 mL) whole wheat flour

1 cup (250 mL) cornmeal

1 cup (250 mL) bread flour

1 cup (250 mL) low sodium chicken stock

½ cup (125 mL) whole milk

1 cup (250 mL) crispy bacon bits (see page 13), with bacon fat from the tray

2 egg yolks

1 cup (250 mL) unsalted butter, melted

— *chapter 2* —

BUTTER

BUTTER

BUTTER—THAT BEAUTIFUL fat made from churned cream. Typically produced from cows, it can also be made with cream from goats, sheep, camels, and buffalo.

In this book, we are only using unsalted butter made from cow's milk. I find salted butter in grocery stores to be overly salted, which can affect your baked goods. Using unsalted butter lets you control the amount of salt you want to put in your recipes, and it leaves you free to choose the kind of salt you want to use in your recipe, whether kosher or sea salt. Also, most commercial salted butters are seasoned with a brine rather than actual sea salt.

The only time I would encourage you to play and experiment with salted butter is when it has been artisanally crafted. It might be a bit more expensive, but the quality of butter made with real sea salt is a dream to play with.

BROWN BUTTER

{ MAKES ½ CUP (125 ML) UNSALTED BUTTER }

The nutty aroma of brown butter, with its light caramel tones, is a magical addition that will enhance the flavours of many recipes. In a soup, mashed potato or cookie recipe, the addition of brown butter adds a unique extra layer of flavour.

INGREDIENTS

1 cup (250 mL) unsalted butter

INSTRUCTIONS In a medium saucepan, melt the butter over low heat. As the butter starts to melt, it will begin to foam and the water content will start to evaporate. The melting butter will change to a light golden colour and browned milk parts will start dropping to the bottom of the saucepan.

At this point, keep a close eye on it. After a minute or two, the colour will darken and a hazelnut aroma will develop. Remove pan from the heat and let it cool at room temperature.

Once cooled, pass the melted brown butter through a fine mesh sieve to remove any burnt bits. Store in an airtight container in the refrigerator.

NOTE: Be careful not to go past the light-brown colour stage or the butter will start to burn. If that happens, remove the saucepan from the stove immediately and allow to cool.

ASSORTED COMPOUND BUTTERS

{EACH RECIPE MAKES 1 CUP (250 ML) BUTTER}

Compound butters are a great and fancy way to enhance the flavour of meat or fish. Kept in the freezer, you just need to slice off what you need for the dish you are preparing. Let the butter slowly melt on a piece of just-grilled beef, on the top of sautéed vegetables or simply spread on toasted multigrain bread.

TARRAGON AND ROASTED GARLIC BUTTER

INSTRUCTIONS In a small roasting pan, combine the peeled garlic and olive oil. Cover with tin foil and cook in a 360°F (180°C) oven for about 25 minutes, until the garlic is soft and slightly browned. Remove from the oven and allow to cool.

In an electric mixing bowl with the paddle attachment, mix the butter on low speed until soft and creamy. Use a rubber spatula to scrape down the sides of the bowl. Add the cooked garlic, dried tarragon and sea salt to the soft butter and mix on low speed for 1 minute.

Transfer the butter to a piece of 20 × 10–inch (50 × 25 cm) parchment paper, then roll into a log about 2 inches (5 cm) in diameter. Refrigerate for 3 hours, then store in the freezer until needed.

INGREDIENTS

½ cup (125 mL) softened unsalted butter

6 cloves of peeled garlic

¼ cup (60 mL) extra virgin olive oil

2 Tbsp (30 mL) dried tarragon

¼ tsp (1 mL) sea salt

DRIED FIG AND CRANBERRY BUTTER

INSTRUCTIONS In an electric mixing bowl with the paddle attachment, mix the butter on low speed until soft and creamy. Use a rubber spatula to scrape down the sides of the bowl.

Remove the tip of each dried fig with a chef's knife and cut into quarters. Chop the dried cranberries into small pieces. Add the figs, dried cranberries and sea salt to the creamy butter and mix for 1 minute on low speed.

Transfer the butter to a piece of 20 × 10–inch (50 × 25 cm) parchment paper, then roll into a log about 2 inches (5 cm) in diameter. Refrigerate for 3 hours, then store in the freezer until needed.

INGREDIENTS

½ cup (125 mL) softened unsalted butter

½ cup (125 mL) dried figs

½ cup (125 mL) dried cranberries

¼ tsp (1 mL) sea salt

. . . Assorted Compound Butters (cont.)

BASIL AND SUNDRIED TOMATO BUTTER

INSTRUCTIONS In an electric mixing bowl with the paddle attachment, mix the butter on low speed until soft and creamy. Use a rubber spatula to scrape down the sides of the bowl.

Stack the basil leaves on top of each other, then carefully cut them into thin strips with a chef's knife and set aside. Cut the sundried tomatoes into thin strips. Add the sliced tomatoes, lemon zest, thyme, sea salt and basil to the creamy butter. Mix for 1 minute.

Transfer the butter to a piece of 20 × 10–inch (50 × 25 cm) parchment paper, then roll into a log about 2 inches (5 cm) in diameter. Refrigerate for 3 hours, then store in the freezer until needed.

INGREDIENTS

½ cup (125 mL) softened unsalted butter

6 medium-size fresh basil leaves

½ cup (125 mL) sundried tomatoes

Zest of 1 lemon

½ tsp (2.5 mL) dried thyme

½ tsp (2.5 mL) sea salt

PORT AND SHALLOT BUTTER

INSTRUCTIONS In an electric mixing bowl with the paddle attachment, mix the butter on low speed until soft and creamy. Use a rubber spatula to scrape down the sides of the bowl.

In a medium saucepan, add the shallots, olive oil, thyme and salt. Cook for 10 minutes over low heat, until the shallots are soft. Stir in the port and continue to cook over low heat for another 10 minutes, occasionally stirring with a wooden spoon. Remove from heat and set aside to cool completely.

Add the shallot mixture to the creamy butter and mix for 1 minute.

Transfer the butter to a piece of 20 × 10–inch (50 × 25 cm) parchment paper, then roll into a log about 2 inches (5 cm) in diameter. Refrigerate for 3 hours, then store in the freezer until needed.

INGREDIENTS

¾ cup (180 mL) softened unsalted butter

¼ cup (60 mL) diced shallots

2 Tbsp (30 mL) extra virgin olive oil

1 tsp (5 mL) chopped fresh thyme

½ tsp (2.5 mL) sea salt

¾ cup (180 mL) port wine

. . . Assorted Compound Butters (cont.)

DRIED PORCINI AND WHITE TRUFFLE OIL BUTTER

INGREDIENTS

¾ cup (180 mL) softened unsalted butter

½ cup (125 mL) dried porcini mushrooms

½ tsp (2.5 mL) sea salt

1 tsp (5 mL) white truffle oil

INSTRUCTIONS In an electric mixing bowl with the paddle attachment, mix the butter on low speed until soft and creamy. Use a rubber spatula to scrape down the sides of the bowl.

Using a chef's knife, chop the dried mushrooms into small pieces. Add the mushrooms, sea salt and truffle oil to the creamy butter and mix for 1 minute.

Transfer the butter to a piece of 20 × 10–inch (50 × 25 cm) parchment paper, then roll into a log about 2 inches (5 cm) in diameter. Refrigerate for 3 hours, then store in the freezer until needed.

SMOKED SALMON AND CHIVE BUTTER

INGREDIENTS

½ cup (125 mL) softened unsalted butter

½ cup (125 mL) diced smoked salmon

2 Tbsp (30 mL) chopped chives

¼ tsp (1 mL) fresh ground black pepper

INSTRUCTIONS In an electric mixing bowl with the paddle attachment, mix the butter on low speed until soft and creamy. Use a rubber spatula to scrape down the sides of the bowl.

Add the smoked salmon, chives and black pepper to the soft butter and mix for 1 minute.

Transfer the butter to a piece of 20 × 10–inch (50 × 25 cm) parchment paper, then roll into a log about 2 inches (5 cm) in diameter. Refrigerate for 3 hours, then store in the freezer until needed.

VERY BUTTERY BRIOCHE

{ MAKES 1 LOAF }

Brioche is a fluffy yet rich and delicate dough that translates into a heavenly food experience. Slice and slather it with butter and jam, or soak it in a custard to make delicious French toast or a pudding.

STARTER

½ cup (125 mL) warm milk

1½ tsp (7.5 mL) instant yeast

1 Tbsp (15 mL) granulated sugar

3 Tbsp (45 mL) bread flour

BRIOCHE

2½ cups (625 mL) bread flour

1 Tbsp (15 mL) granulated sugar

1 tsp (5 mL) sea salt

¾ cup (180 mL) diced cold unsalted butter

4 large eggs, divided

1 egg yolk

INSTRUCTIONS FOR STARTER In a small saucepan, warm the milk to about 104°F (41°C). Whisk in the instant yeast, sugar and flour until the mixture is smooth. Cover the saucepan with plastic wrap and rest in a warm place for the yeast to activate, about 20 minutes.

INSTRUCTIONS FOR BRIOCHE In an electric mixing bowl with the hook attachment, stir together the flour, sugar and salt on low speed for 1 minute.

Once the yeast is activated, it will start to bubble. Add it to the flour along with the butter, 3 eggs and the yolk. Mix on low speed for about 20 minutes until the dough comes together around the hook and the butter blends into the dough. Remove the hook and cover the bowl with plastic wrap. Refrigerate overnight.

The next day, turn the dough out onto a lightly floured work surface and divide into 4 equal portions. Shape each portion into a ball, then place the balls side-by-side in a nonstick loaf pan and cover the pan with a clean towel. Place the pan in a warm area to allow the brioche dough to proof for about 2 hours and double in volume.

Preheat oven to 370°F (185°C).

Once the dough has doubled in size, beat the remaining egg and delicately brush the egg wash overtop. Bake for 40 minutes or until the top of the brioche has a beautiful light golden colour. Let it cool on a rack, then unmould.

When cool, the brioche can be wrapped in plastic and frozen until needed.

CAULIFLOWER SOUP

{ MAKES 4 SERVINGS }

This is one of the most aromatic soups I have ever made. It is silky, creamy, nutty, buttery and slightly herbaceous. It is delicious warm, but also served chilled.

INSTRUCTIONS Preheat oven to 350°F (175°C).

Remove the green leaves around the base of the cauliflower and cut the head into small pieces. Place half the cauliflower pieces on a parchment-lined baking tray, drizzle with 2 Tbsp (30 mL) extra virgin olive oil and bake in the oven for 30 minutes.

In a large pot, warm the remaining olive oil over medium heat. Add the chopped onion and cook, stirring with a wooden spoon, until the onion is slightly brown in colour. Add the garlic, sherry vinegar, thyme, rosemary and the other half of the cauliflower. Keep stirring with a wooden spoon until the cauliflower starts to brown.

Add the vegetable stock and whipping cream and cook for about 20 minutes over low heat.

Add salt and pepper to taste. Remove pot from heat and let cool.

Once the soup is cool, blend in the brown butter with a tall handheld blender until smooth. Serve soup cold or warm it up again in a pot before serving. Sprinkle chopped chives overtop.

INGREDIENTS

1 head cauliflower

¼ cup (60 mL) extra virgin olive oil, divided

1 cup (250 mL) chopped yellow onion

2 Tbsp (30 mL) chopped garlic

2 Tbsp (30 mL) sherry vinegar

2 tsp (10 mL) chopped thyme

2 tsp (10 mL) chopped rosemary

4 cups (1 L) low sodium vegetable stock

1 cup (250 mL) whipping cream

Salt and pepper to taste

½ cup (125 mL) melted brown butter (see page 52)

2 tsp (10 mL) chopped chives for serving

BUTTER AND SOY-GLAZED BRUSSELS SPROUTS

{ MAKES 4 SERVINGS }

Brussels sprouts are a vegetable people love to hate, but they are so easy to cook and transform into a delicious side dish. Blending butter and soy sauce is magical—it creates a silky and delicate umami flavour. There is no salt added to this recipe. The saltiness comes from the soy sauce.

INGREDIENTS

1 lb (500 g) Brussels sprouts, washed and cut into halves

3 Tbsp (45 mL) extra virgin olive oil

1 Tbsp (15 mL) honey

3 Tbsp (45 mL) soy sauce

Fresh ground black pepper to taste

3 Tbsp (45 mL) unsalted butter

1 tsp (5 mL) fresh chopped garlic

1 Tbsp (15 mL) chopped parsley for serving

INSTRUCTIONS Preheat oven to 360°F (180°C).

In a medium bowl, toss the Brussels sprout halves with the olive oil, honey, soy sauce and black pepper. Spread the Brussels sprouts on a parchment-lined baking tray and place in the oven. Bake for 40 minutes, until the sprouts are slightly charred and soft.

Remove baked sprouts from the oven and place in a sauté pan over low heat. Add 1 Tbsp (15 mL) water, the butter and the chopped garlic and cook for about 1 minute while stirring.

Remove sprouts and place in a serving dish. Sprinkle with chopped parsley and serve.

HERB AND BUTTER-ROASTED HEIRLOOM CARROTS

{ MAKES 4 SERVINGS }

Combining the natural sweetness of these heirloom carrots with a "bath" of butter allows their authentic flavour to shine through. To preserve even more of that authenticity, I suggest leaving the peel intact. I have never peeled carrots. It is not necessary, and it creates unwanted food waste. Just give them a nice wash—the peel gives them a beautiful rustic look.

INGREDIENTS

1 dozen organic heirloom carrots

2 Tbsp (30 mL) extra virgin olive oil

½ tsp (2.5 mL) chopped garlic

½ tsp (2.5 mL) chopped thyme

½ tsp (2.5 mL) chopped rosemary

Salt and pepper to taste

½ cup (125 mL) unsalted butter

1 tsp (5 mL) chopped chives for serving

INSTRUCTIONS Preheat oven to 375°F (190°C).

Clip the carrot tops but leave about 1 inch (2.5 cm) of the stems. Wash the carrots under cold water and cut in half lengthwise, then place in a large bowl and toss with the olive oil, garlic, thyme, rosemary, salt and pepper to taste.

Arrange the carrots on a parchment-lined baking tray. Crumble the butter into small pieces overtop of the carrots. Place the tray in the oven and bake for about 40 minutes.

Serve carrots in the baking tray or transfer to a suitable dish. Sprinkle with chopped chives. Allow to cool slightly before serving.

GRILLED RIBEYE STEAK WITH BÉARNAISE SAUCE

{ MAKES 2 SERVINGS }

Béarnaise is an emulsion sauce in the same family as a traditional hollandaise sauce, but I find béarnaise creamier and a bit punchier, and I love the uniqueness of using tarragon as an herb. Béarnaise sauce is good on so many dishes like meat and fish, but also simply on roasted potatoes or grilled asparagus.

BÉARNAISE SAUCE

1 cup + 30 mL (280 mL) unsalted butter, divided

2 Tbsp (30 mL) white wine vinegar

1 Tbsp (15 mL) lemon juice

2 Tbsp (30 mL) chopped shallots

3 large egg yolks

¼ tsp (1 mL) cayenne pepper

½ tsp (2.5 mL) thyme

Salt and pepper to taste

1 Tbsp (15 mL) chopped tarragon

STEAK

Salt and pepper to taste

1 ribeye steak

INSTRUCTIONS FOR BÉARNAISE SAUCE In a small saucepan, warm 2 Tbsp (30 mL) butter over medium heat. Add the chopped shallots and cook for 1 minute. Add the vinegar and lemon juice and cook for 1 more minute. Pour the mixture into a tall blender.

Melt the remaining 1 cup (250 mL) butter and set aside.

Add the egg yolks to the blender and mix on medium speed. Slowly pour in the melted butter until the mixture starts to emulsify. Add the cayenne pepper, thyme and salt and pepper to taste. Once the sauce is blended into a thick and creamy texture, pour into a small serving bowl and mix in the tarragon. Set aside at room temperature for 20 minutes before serving.

INSTRUCTIONS FOR STEAK Sprinkle salt and pepper on both sides of the ribeye steak. Grill the steak over a high temperature (450°F/230°C), making certain that each side of the steak is grilled to a beautiful char and the desired temperature. Let it rest for 5 minutes then slice and place on a serving platter. Serve with the béarnaise sauce on top or on the side.

GRILLED SHRIMP WITH CAYENNE PEPPER BUTTER

{ MAKES 4 SERVINGS }

I prefer using shrimp with their heads and shells attached for an enhanced flavour experience. Grilling the crustacean shells adds a lot of extra flavours, and while it is for sure messier to eat, the shell helps protect the lean and delicate shrimp flesh during cooking, making it juicy and tender.

INGREDIENTS

½ cup (125 mL) unsalted butter

½ tsp (2.5 mL) cayenne pepper

12 large shrimp

½ cup (125 mL) extra virgin olive oil + 1 tsp (5 mL) for the pan

1 tsp (5 mL) chopped garlic

2 Tbsp (30 mL) fish sauce

1 tsp (5 mL) chopped parsley

Salt and pepper to taste

INSTRUCTIONS Preheat oven to 375°F (190°C).

In a small saucepan, melt the butter and whisk in the cayenne pepper.

In a medium bowl, toss together the shrimp, ½ cup (125 mL) olive oil, garlic, fish sauce, parsley and salt and pepper to taste. Set aside.

Heat a cast iron pan over medium heat. Add 1 tsp (5 mL) olive oil, then, using a pair of tongs, place the shrimp in the hot pan and cook for 1 minute per side.

Transfer the shrimp to a parchment-lined baking tray. Drizzle the shrimp with the cayenne butter and bake for 10 minutes. Serve while still hot.

GOOEY BROWN-BUTTER LEMON COOKIES

{ MAKES 12 COOKIES }

The last time I made these delicious gooey cookies with my son, they never had a chance to make it into the cookie tin. The cookies were all devoured within minutes after they cooled. As my son would say, "We are cookie monsters!"

INGREDIENTS

¾ cup (180 mL) cream cheese

½ cup (125 mL) softened unsalted butter

¼ cup (60 mL) light brown sugar

¼ tsp (1 mL) sea salt

2 egg yolks

1 cup (250 mL) yellow cake mix (store-bought)

Zest of 1 lemon

½ cup (125 mL) brown butter (see page 52), melted

¼ cup (60 mL) icing sugar

INSTRUCTIONS Preheat oven to 350°F (175°C).

In an electric mixing bowl with the paddle attachment, cream together the cream cheese, butter and brown sugar on low speed. While mixing, add the sea salt and egg yolks. Scrape down the sides of the bowl to ensure the mixture is free of cream cheese lumps. Add the yellow cake mix, lemon zest and brown butter and mix on low speed until well blended.

Using a soup spoon, roll perfectly round cookie balls about 1 inch (2.5 cm) in diameter and place them on the baking tray, spacing them about 2 inches (5 cm) apart from each other. Using a small sieve, sprinkle each cookie with a generous amount of icing sugar.

Place the cookies in the oven and bake for 11 minutes, then remove and place on a cooling rack. Store in an airtight container at room temperature up to 2 weeks.

LOUISVILLE BUTTER CAKE

{ MAKES ONE 10-INCH (25 CM) BUNDT CAKE }

An old fashioned moist and utterly buttery cake, the Louisville is easy to make and so delicious. I always drizzle a wonderful vanilla bourbon glaze on top or serve it warm with a scoop of vanilla ice cream that melts into the cake.

LOUISVILLE BUTTER CAKE

3 cups (750 mL) all-purpose flour

1 cup (250 mL) granulated sugar

1 cup (250 mL) light brown sugar

1 tsp (5 mL) baking powder

½ tsp (2.5 mL) baking soda

½ tsp (2.5 mL) sea salt

1 cup (250 mL) buttermilk

¼ cup (60 mL) honey

1 tsp (5 mL) vanilla extract

5 large eggs

1½ cups (375 mL) melted unsalted butter

VANILLA BOURBON GLAZE (OPTIONAL)

½ cup (125 mL) unsalted butter

½ cup (125 mL) orange juice

1 tsp (5 mL) vanilla extract

3 Tbsp (45 mL) bourbon

1 cup (250 mL) icing sugar

INSTRUCTIONS FOR LOUISVILLE BUTTER CAKE Preheat oven to 360°F (180°C).

In an electric mixing bowl with the paddle attachment, mix the flour, sugars, baking powder, baking soda and sea salt for 2 minutes.

In a medium bowl, whisk together the buttermilk, honey, vanilla extract and eggs. Stir in the melted butter. Pour the liquid mixture into the flour mixture and mix on low speed until just incorporated. Do not overmix the batter.

Pour the batter into a nonstick Bundt cake mould and bake for about 60 minutes. Once baked, the tip of a knife or a toothpick inserted into the centre of the cake should come out clean.

INSTRUCTIONS FOR VANILLA BOURBON GLAZE (OPTIONAL) In a medium saucepan, melt the butter over low heat. Remove from heat, then whisk in the orange juice, vanilla extract, bourbon and icing sugar and stir until smooth. Pass through a fine mesh sieve into a container and set aside until ready to drizzle on the cake. Any excess glaze can be refrigerated up to 5 days.

ASSEMBLY Remove cake from the oven and place on a cooling rack. The cake must be completely cool before flipping the mould onto a serving plate to release it. Serve with vanilla bourbon glaze or ice cream.

BROWN BUTTER APPLE FUDGE

{ MAKES 36 SQUARES }

I've always loved the rustic appeal of fudge. With a texture somewhere between caramel and fondant, it's a great platform for creativity. Adding some cardamom to this recipe brings an aromatic depth to the bright flavour of the green apple.

INSTRUCTIONS FOR APPLE SAUCE In a medium saucepan, cook the diced apple, butter, brown sugar, cardamom and salt over low heat, stirring from time to time. Cook for about 15 minutes, until the texture turns into a compote. Set aside in the refrigerator until needed.

INSTRUCTIONS FOR FUDGE In a large saucepan, stir together both sugars, the condensed milk and the brown butter; bring to a simmer over low heat while continuously stirring with a wooden spoon. Reduce heat to low and continue cooking for about 20 minutes, until the mixture thickens and becomes darker in colour. Add the apple sauce and cook over low heat for another 10 minutes while continuously stirring with a wooden spoon. The fudge texture should be gooey.

Transfer the fudge to a greased parchment-lined baking tray and place on a cooling rack to rest for at least 3 hours.

Cut the fudge into 2 × 2-inch (5 × 5 cm) squares. Store in an airtight container in a cool place up to 1 month.

APPLE SAUCE

3 green apples, peeled, cored and diced into ¼-inch (0.6 cm) cubes

¼ cup (60 mL) softened unsalted butter

¼ cup (60 mL) light brown sugar

¼ tsp (1 mL) ground cardamom

¼ tsp (1 mL) sea salt

FUDGE

2 cups (500 mL) granulated sugar

¼ cup (60 mL) light brown sugar

3 cups (750 mL) condensed milk

¼ cup (60 mL) melted brown butter (see page 52)

SPECULAAS COOKIES

{ MAKES 36 COOKIES }

This is a wonderful cookie recipe to make and enjoy. It has its origin in Holland, but is also found in Belgium, northern France and Germany. The blend of spices is a sensory reminder that the holidays are always just around the corner, no matter what time of year it is. The dough does not rise much, so it is important to roll it thin for that perfect crispy and slightly chewy texture.

INGREDIENTS

½ cup (125 mL) hazelnut flour

1½ cups (375 mL) all-purpose flour

½ tsp (2.5 mL) baking soda

¼ tsp (1 mL) sea salt

½ tsp (2.5 mL) ground cinnamon

½ tsp (2.5 mL) ground ginger

¼ tsp (1 mL) ground cardamom

¼ tsp (1 mL) ground coriander

¼ tsp (1 mL) ground nutmeg

½ cup (125 mL) unsalted butter

½ cup (125 mL) light brown sugar

½ cup (125 mL) granulated sugar

1 large egg

1 egg yolk

INSTRUCTIONS In a medium bowl, stir together the flours, baking soda, salt and all of the spices.

In an electric mixing bowl with the paddle attachment, beat the butter and both sugars on low speed. Use a rubber spatula to scrape down the sides of the bowl. Continue mixing on low speed then add the egg and egg yolk. Mix until fully incorporated. Add the flour mixture and blend at low speed until the dough comes together.

Turn the dough out onto a lightly floured work surface. Finish mixing the dough by hand then flatten it into a ½-inch (1 cm) thick rectangle. Wrap in plastic wrap and refrigerate for at least 4 hours.

Preheat oven to 360°F (180°C).

Remove dough from the fridge and unwrap. Roll on a floured surface until ⅛ inch (3 mm) thick. Cut out shapes using animal-shaped cookie cutters (if you have them, otherwise just cut into circles) and place the cut cookies on a parchment-lined baking tray, spacing the cookies 1 inch (2.5 cm) apart from each other. Bake for 10 minutes until the edges are a light golden colour.

Transfer to cooling rack. Once cooled, store in an airtight container up to 1 month.

BROWN BUTTER SCHNECKENNUDELS

{ MAKE 24 COOKIES }

My maternal grandpa Hans, who was born in Berlin, called these delicious, easy-to-make cookies "schneckennudels." We would bake them on wintery days and enjoy them with hot chocolate. Grandpa Hans knew his cookies. On the other hand, he also loved eating cold spaghetti with strawberry jam.

INSTRUCTIONS In an electric mixing bowl with the paddle attachment, blend together the sugars, flour, salt, baking soda and cornstarch. Add the egg, egg yolk and brown butter and mix on low speed until the dough comes together.

Roll the dough into walnut-size balls and place on a parchment-lined baking tray. Freeze for 30 minutes.

Preheat oven to 360°F (180°C).

In a small bowl, stir together the icing sugar and cinnamon. Remove tray from the freezer and coat each ball with egg white then roll in the sugar and cinnamon mixture.

Place dough balls on a parchment-lined baking tray, spacing the balls 2 inches (5 cm) apart from each other. Bake for 10 minutes, until the tops start to brown and crack.

Remove from the oven and place on a cooling rack; cookies should be soft in the centre. Once cooled, store cookies in an airtight container in a cool place up to 1 month.

INGREDIENTS

½ cup (125 mL) light brown sugar

½ cup (125 mL) granulated sugar

1½ cups (375 mL) all-purpose flour

¼ tsp (1 mL) sea salt

½ tsp (2.5 mL) baking soda

1 tsp (5 mL) cornstarch

1 large egg

1 egg yolk

½ cup (125 mL) melted brown butter (see page 52)

¼ cup (60 mL) icing sugar

1 tsp (5 mL) ground cinnamon

1 large egg white

BROWN BUTTER AND WHITE CHOCOLATE CHIP COOKIES

{ MAKES 24 COOKIES }

The best kept secret in making a great chocolate chip cookie is to make the dough a day ahead and let it rest overnight in the fridge. The second best kept secret is to use brown butter for extra flavour. This recipe will not disappoint the baker seeking chocolate chip cookie perfection. For better results, prepare the dough 1 day before baking the cookies.

INGREDIENTS

2 cups (500 mL) all-purpose flour

1 cup (250 mL) light brown sugar

½ cup (125 mL) granulated sugar

1 tsp (5 mL) baking soda

½ tsp (2.5 mL) ground cardamom

½ tsp (2.5 mL) sea salt

½ cup (125 mL) melted brown butter (see page 52)

1 tsp (5 mL) vanilla extract

2 large eggs

1 egg yolk

1¼ cups (310 mL) white chocolate chips

INSTRUCTIONS In a large bowl, stir together the flour, sugars, baking soda, ground cardamom and sea salt. Transfer the dry ingredients to an electric mixing bowl fitted with the paddle attachment. Mix in the brown butter, vanilla extract, eggs and egg yolk on low speed until the dough comes together. Add the chocolate chips and mix for 1 minute. The dough will be a bit soft but will firm somewhat once the butter starts to solidify. Wrap in plastic and let it set in the fridge overnight.

The next day, preheat oven to 360°F (180°C).

Using an ice cream scoop, shape the cookies into small round balls and place on a baking tray, spacing the balls 2.5 inches (6 cm) apart from each other. Bake for 8 minutes, until the edges are golden brown but the centres are still soft.

Cool on a wire rack. Store cookies in an airtight container at room temperature up to 1 month.

BROWN BUTTER APPLE CRUMBLE PIE

{ MAKES ONE 9-INCH (23 CM) PIE }

Simplicity is what makes a perfect apple pie. I've done a lot of homework to create the perfect pie filling—from the types of apples to use, to the perfect amount of sugar—but one thing is for sure. Adding brown butter makes an amazing apple pie.

APPLE FILLING

4 Gala apples, peeled, cored and diced into ½-inch (1 cm) cubes

1 cup (250 mL) canned apple filling

¼ cup (60 mL) cold brown butter (see page 52)

½ cup (125 mL) diced dried apple

½ cup (125 mL) light brown sugar

¼ cup (60 mL) granulated sugar

1 tsp (5 mL) cornstarch

¼ cup (60 mL) apple juice

1 tsp (5 mL) vanilla extract

PIE DOUGH

1¾ cups (430 mL) all-purpose flour

½ tsp (2.5 mL) sea salt

½ cup (125 mL) diced cold unsalted butter

2 Tbsp (30 mL) whole milk

½ cup (125 mL) cold water

. . . ingredients continued

INSTRUCTIONS FOR APPLE FILLING In a medium saucepan, cook the diced apple, canned apple filling, brown butter, dried apple, and brown sugar over medium heat until simmering.

In a small bowl, stir together the sugar and cornstarch, then whisk it into the simmering apple filling. Add the apple juice and vanilla extract. Bring to a boil and cook for 2 minutes while stirring with a wooden spoon. Set aside and let it cool.

Apple filling can be made a few days ahead and refrigerated.

INSTRUCTIONS FOR PIE DOUGH In an electric mixing bowl with the paddle attachment, mix the flour, salt and diced cold butter on low speed until the butter disappears. Add the milk and water and continue mixing until the dough comes together. Do not overmix.

Turn the dough out onto a floured work surface and shape into a 1-inch (2.5 cm) thick rectangular brick. Wrap in plastic and refrigerate for 3 hours.

. . . recipe continued

CRUMBLE TOPPING

½ cup (125 mL) cold unsalted butter

¾ cup (180 mL) granulated sugar

1 tsp (5 mL) vanilla extract

½ cup (125 mL) bread flour

¾ cup (180 mL) cake flour

¼ tsp (1 mL) sea salt

Whipped cream or ice cream for serving

INSTRUCTIONS FOR CRUMBLE TOPPING In an electric mixing bowl with the paddle attachment, cream together the butter and sugar on low speed. Use a rubber spatula to scrape down the sides of the bowl and ensure there are no lumps. Add the vanilla extract then both flours. Mix on low speed until the dough just comes together. Do not overmix.

Pass the dough through a large mesh rack onto a parchment-lined baking tray to create ¼-inch (0.5 cm) crumbs. Place tray in the refrigerator for 2 hours. Once cold, the crumble topping should be handled delicately and kept cold to maintain its shape. Refrigerate in an airtight container until needed.

ASSEMBLY Preheat oven to 360°F (180°C).

Remove dough from the refrigerator and roll into a ⅛-inch (3 mm) round shape that's large enough to overlap the pie pan by 1 inch (2.5 cm). Place the pastry in a 9-inch (23 cm) pie pan and fill with the apple mixture. Crumble the topping overtop and gently press down to create a seal between the pie dough and crumble topping. Trim the excess pie dough with a small knife.

Bake for about 25 minutes or until the topping is golden brown and the apple filling starts to slightly bubble out. Serve lukewarm with whipped cream or ice cream.

BROWN BUTTER BLUEBERRY BAKEWELL TART

{ MAKES ONE 10-INCH (25 CM) ROUND TART }

A classic British dessert with a French twist and a jam filling made of delicious blueberries. One great thing about a Bakewell tart is that you can bake it well in advance and store in the freezer until needed.

ALMOND PATE SABLÉE

¾ cup (180 mL) diced cold unsalted butter

½ tsp (2.5 mL) sea salt

2 cups (500 mL) cake flour

¾ cup (180 mL) icing sugar

¼ cup (60 mL) ground almonds

1 large egg, beaten

BROWN BUTTER FRANGIPANE

¼ cup (60 mL) softened brown butter (see page 52)

½ cup (125 mL) granulated sugar

¼ cup (60 mL) brown sugar

1 large egg

¾ cup (180 mL) ground almonds

¾ cup (180 mL) all-purpose flour

½ tsp (2.5 mL) sea salt

INSTRUCTIONS FOR ALMOND PATE SABLÉE In an electric mixing bowl with the paddle attachment, mix the butter, salt and flour on low speed until it resembles small crumbs. Add the icing sugar and ground almonds and mix for 1 minute. Add the egg and continue mixing at low speed until the dough comes together.

Turn the dough out onto a lightly floured work surface and finish combining it with your hands. Shape into a ½-inch (1 cm) thick brick, wrap in plastic and refrigerate for 1 hour. The dough can be made days ahead.

INSTRUCTIONS FOR BROWN BUTTER FRANGIPANE In an electric mixing bowl with the paddle attachment, mix the brown butter and both sugars together on low speed. Scrape down the sides of the bowl to ensure the mixture is free of lumps. Stop the mixer, add the egg and mix again at low speed until fully incorporated. Add ground almonds, flour and salt. Resume mixing on low speed until the dough comes together. Set aside and maintain at room temperature until ready to assemble the tart.

INSTRUCTIONS FOR BLUEBERRY JAM In a medium saucepan, bring the blueberries and sugar to a simmer over low heat. In a small bowl, stir together the cornstarch and cold water, then add to simmering blueberry mixture. Add the lemon zest and bring to a boil. Cook for 3 minutes, continuously stirring with a wooden spoon.

Remove saucepan from heat and cool until needed. The jam can be made days ahead and stored in a refrigerated airtight container until needed.

ASSEMBLY Roll the dough to a ⅛-inch (3 mm) thick circle with a 13-inch (33 cm) diameter and place in a tart mould. Trim the excess dough and refrigerate the tart shell for 30 minutes.

Preheat oven to 360°F (180°C).

Once chilled, prick the entire surface of the shell with a fork. Line the bottom with a piece of parchment paper and fill with pie weights or uncooked beans. Blind bake for 20 minutes, then remove from the oven and set aside to cool.

Spread the blueberry jam ¼-inch (0.5 cm) thick over the base of the tart. Gently spread the soft brown butter frangipane overtop, carefully sealing the jam between the tart shell and the layer of frangipane. Freeze for 1 hour.

Dust a generous amount of icing sugar on the top of the tart and bake for 40 minutes (still at 360°F/180°C) while still frozen, until the top is light golden with slightly darker edges.

Remove from the oven and place on a cooling rack. While still hot, dust the top with more icing sugar. Remove from the tart mould and place on a platter, ready to serve.

BLUEBERRY JAM

1½ cups (375 mL) fresh or frozen blueberries

1½ cups (375 mL) granulated sugar

1 Tbsp (15 mL) cornstarch

2 tsp (10 mL) cold water

Zest of 1 lemon

¼ cup (60 mL) icing sugar for the top

BUTTER TARTS . . . WITH RAISINS

{ MAKES TWELVE 3-INCH (8 CM) TARTS }

A quintessential Canadian treat, this butter tart recipe comes from an old family friend. For many years, the innocent butter tart has sparked an ongoing nation-wide culinary debate: raisins or no raisins? Within families, clans of "for or against" have formed—even friends and colleagues offer up opinions. As for me, I say keep the raisins, add some bourbon, and just enjoy these sweet, gooey treats. The key to a perfect butter tart? Do not overbake them.

INGREDIENTS

1½ cups (375 mL) golden raisins

¾ cup (180 mL) unsalted butter

1½ cups (375 mL) light brown sugar

2 large eggs

¼ cup (60 mL) buttermilk

1 tsp (5 mL) vanilla extract

¼ cup (60 mL) bourbon

12 unbaked tart shells (use store-bought frozen shells)

INSTRUCTIONS In a medium saucepan, boil 2 cups (500 mL) water. Remove from heat and add the golden raisins to the water. Let the raisins soak for 30 minutes.

Melt the butter over low heat and set aside at room temperature.

In a medium bowl, mix together the light brown sugar and eggs using a medium hand whisk. Add the melted butter, buttermilk, vanilla extract and bourbon and mix until fully incorporated.

Place the wet raisins in a sieve to drain the excess water, then place into a small bowl. Add the bourbon to the raisins and let soak for 15 minutes.

Preheat oven to 340°F (170°C).

Place the tart shells on a baking tray. Divide the raisins between the 12 unbaked tart shells. Pour the butter tart filling over the raisins up to the top of each shell. Bake for about 25 minutes, until the edges of the tarts become a light golden colour.

Remove tarts from the oven and place on a cooling rack. Once cooled, transfer to an airtight container and store at room temperature. Tarts are good up to 3 days, if they can last that long without being eaten.

This recipe will finally put to rest that great culinary debate for good.

— *chapter 3* —

BOURBON

BOURBON

DEEPLY ASSOCIATED WITH Kentucky, bourbon is made primarily from corn and aged in new charred oak barrels that give it its unique flavours.

I prefer baking and cooking with bourbon rather than other whiskeys, which can be too strong and "harsh." Bourbons are more melodious in terms of flavour. Bourbon also has a long history associated with baking in Kentucky, Alabama, Tennessee, and Mississippi.

No need to spend a lot of money when cooking with bourbon. Jim Bean is perfect.

BOURBON GARLIC GLAZED YAMS

{ MAKES 2 SERVINGS }

This savoury dish truly borders on being a dessert. You could be daring and serve it as the finale to a feast, or as a beautiful complement to roasted or braised meats as part of a main course. It's perfect for a holiday gathering or even during barbecue season.

INSTRUCTIONS Preheat oven to 350°F (175°C).

Peel the yams and cut them into 3-inch (8 cm) long, ½-inch (1 cm) wide sticks. Place the yam sticks in a large bowl and then add olive oil, salt, orange zest, honey, garlic, sambal oelek, rosemary, bourbon and black pepper to taste. Toss everything together.

Place the coated yams in a ceramic roasting pan and bake for 20 minutes, then remove from the oven. Break the butter into small pieces and sprinkle on top of the yams. Return to the oven for another 20 minutes or until the yams are soft and the edges are slightly dark.

INGREDIENTS

3 medium yams

2 Tbsp (30 mL) extra virgin olive oil

½ tsp (2.5 mL) sea salt

Zest of 1 orange

3 Tbsp (45 mL) honey

2 tsp (10 mL) fresh chopped garlic

1 tsp (5 mL) sambal oelek chili sauce

1 tsp (5 mL) fresh chopped rosemary

½ cup (125 mL) bourbon

Fresh ground black pepper to taste

2 Tbsp (30 mL) cold unsalted butter

PORK BELLY WITH BOURBON HONEY GLAZE

{ MAKES 4 SERVINGS }

Pork belly has long been a mainstay in Chinese, Korean and Filipino cuisines, and in recent years it has become a popular menu item in western cuisine too—to the delight of many. That's something to celebrate. We have another delicious way to eat bacon!

PORK BELLY

1 pork belly (about 1¾ lb/800 g)

4 tsp (20 mL) extra virgin olive oil, divided

1 tsp (5 mL) sea salt

1 tsp (5 mL) fresh cracked black pepper

2 Tbsp (30 mL) balsamic vinegar

½ cup (125 mL) low sodium chicken stock

½ cup (125 mL) bourbon

1 piece star anise

BOURBON HONEY GLAZE

½ cup (125 mL) low sodium chicken stock

½ cup (125 mL) bourbon

6 Tbsp (90 mL) tomato ketchup

¼ cup (60 mL) light soy sauce

2 Tbsp (30 mL) hickory barbecue sauce

6 Tbsp (90 mL) honey

¼ cup (60 mL) ponzu sauce

---

2 tsp (10 mL) toasted sesame seeds for serving

1 tsp (5 mL) finely chopped chives for serving

INSTRUCTIONS FOR PORK BELLY Preheat oven to 370°F (185°C).

Rub the top of the pork belly with half of the olive oil. Using a sharp knife, make several parallel cuts ¼ inch (0.5 cm) from each other across the skin of the pork belly. Cut through the skin and fat but not into the meat. Sprinkle the salt and black pepper on the top of the pork belly.

In a medium stainless-steel roasting pan, warm the remaining olive oil over medium heat. Place the pork belly skin-side-down and cook until the skin browns. Turn the pork belly over and add the balsamic vinegar to the pan along with the chicken stock, bourbon and star anise. Bring to a boil over medium heat for 1 minute.

Remove from heat, then cover the entire roasting pan with foil. Bake for 3 hours, then remove the foil and continue baking for 20 minutes at 410°F (210°C). Remove pork belly from the oven and let it rest for 20 minutes at room temperature.

INSTRUCTIONS FOR BOURBON AND HONEY GLAZE In a small saucepan, add the chicken stock, bourbon, ketchup, soy sauce, barbecue sauce, honey and ponzu sauce. Stir well using a small whisk, place on the stove over medium heat and bring to a quick boil. Set aside and allow to cool.

ASSEMBLY Cut the pork belly into 4 equal pieces and place into 4 deep soup or pasta bowls. Spoon the glaze overtop and sprinkle with toasted sesame seeds and chives. Serve with a side of yam purée or your favourite vegetables.

THE WORLD'S No. 1 BOURBON WHISKEY
LE MEILLEUR BOURBON AU MONDE
JIM BEAM
JIM BEAM B SINCE 1795
KENTUCKY STRAIGHT
BOURBON
WHISKEY
PRODUCT OF UNITED STATES / FAIT AUX ÉTATS-UNIS

ROASTED JAPANESE EGGPLANT WITH SWEET BOURBON GLAZE

{ MAKES 4 SERVINGS }

As you drizzle this sweet bourbon glaze over the roasted Japanese eggplant, it is absorbed like a sponge, blending into the eggplant's delicate silky texture and making it oh so appealing for a grown-up palate. The addition of sambal oelek chili sauce right before serving lifts up the flavours.

INSTRUCTIONS FOR ROASTED EGGPLANT Preheat oven to 370°F (185°C).

Slice the eggplants in half lengthwise and, using a small knife, cut shallow crisscross marks into the inside flesh. Brush the cut sides with olive oil and place the eggplant halves on a parchment-lined baking tray. Sprinkle with sea salt.

Bake for 20 minutes until light brown in colour and soft. More time might be necessary depending on the eggplant width.

INSTRUCTIONS FOR SWEET BOURBON GLAZE In a medium saucepan, whisk together the bourbon, brown sugar, Worcestershire sauce, orange juice, honey, apple cider vinegar and garlic. Place on the stove and bring to a boil. Reduce heat to low and cook for another 5 minutes, continuing to stir. Set aside to cool at room temperature.

ASSEMBLY In a sauté pan, toast the white and black sesame seeds over low heat. Toss around the seeds by shaking the pan until the seeds are lightly toasted, then remove from heat and set aside until needed.

Place the 4 baked eggplants on a platter while still hot, then drizzle a generous amount of bourbon glaze overtop and sprinkle with the chopped chives, toasted sesame seeds and sambal oelek. Serve and enjoy.

ROASTED EGGPLANT

4 medium Japanese eggplants

¼ cup (60 mL) extra virgin olive oil

½ tsp (2.5 mL) sea salt

SWEET BOURBON GLAZE

1 cup (250 mL) bourbon

½ cup (125 mL) dark brown sugar

1 Tbsp (15 mL) Worcestershire sauce

½ cup (125 mL) orange juice

2 Tbsp (30 mL) honey

2 Tbsp (30 mL) apple cider vinegar

1 tsp (5 mL) fresh chopped garlic

---

2 Tbsp (30 mL) toasted white sesame seeds for serving

2 tsp (10 mL) toasted black sesame seeds for serving

1 Tbsp (15 mL) chopped chives for serving

2 Tbsp (30 mL) sambal oelek chili sauce for serving

BOURBON MAPLE-GLAZED SOCKEYE SALMON

{ MAKES 4 SALMON FILETS }

Sockeye salmon from the Pacific Northwest is one of nature's most delicious foods, no matter the species: coho, king, sockeye, steelhead or spring. It is truly food of the ocean gods. Its delicate buttery flesh is embellished with the sweetness and slight acidity of this simple-to-make glaze.

INGREDIENTS

1 cup (250 mL) pure maple syrup

½ cup (125 mL) orange juice

Zest of 1 orange

¼ cup (60 mL) bourbon

1 Tbsp (15 mL) dark miso

¼ tsp (1 mL) fresh ground black pepper

¼ tsp (1 mL) sea salt

1 tsp (5 mL) chopped fresh garlic

Four 6 oz (175 g) salmon filets

2 tsp (10 mL) fresh chopped chives for serving

INSTRUCTIONS In a medium saucepan, stir together the maple syrup, orange juice, orange zest, bourbon, miso, black pepper and salt. Warm the mixture over low heat and cook for 15 minutes. Remove saucepan from heat, whisk in the garlic and set aside to cool at room temperature.

Lay the salmon filets in a deep dish and spoon half the cooled glaze over top for it to marinate. Cover with plastic wrap and refrigerate for 2 hours.

Preheat oven to 325°F (150°C).

Remove each salmon piece from the dish and place them in a foil-lined baking tray, spaced out evenly from each other. Spoon a generous amount of the remaining glaze onto each portion of salmon. Bake for 12 minutes, until the glaze starts to brown into a beautiful amber colour.

Remove salmon from the oven and let it rest at room temperature for 10 minutes. To serve, sprinkle with fresh chopped chives. Enjoy with any roasted vegetables.

Canadian Pure
Maple Syrup
250 ml
FRESH & WILD
13.99

BACON BOURBON JAM

{ MAKES 1½ CUPS (375 ML) }

This is what sweet dreams are made of: a full spoon of bacon bourbon jam right before going to bed. It's the perfect blend of sweetness and smokiness with a hint of spice and herbal notes.

INSTRUCTIONS In a medium saucepan, heat the butter over low heat until melted. Add the diced bacon. Stir with a wooden spoon and cook until the bacon is crispy, about 12 minutes.

Transfer the cooked bacon to a fine mesh strainer to drain off fat. Drain the remaining fat from the pan then add the olive oil. Add the diced onion and cook over low heat while continuously stirring with a wooden spoon. Once the onions start to turn a light golden colour, add the salt, brown sugar, honey, cayenne pepper, black pepper, thyme and rosemary. Keep cooking over low heat for 10 minutes.

Add the cooked bacon, orange zest, raspberry vinegar and bourbon. Continue cooking over low heat for 15 minutes or until the mixture achieves a jam consistency. Remove from heat and allow to cool.

Once cool, transfer the jam to an airtight container and store in the refrigerator up to 1 month.

INGREDIENTS

3 Tbsp (45 mL) unsalted butter

2 lb (900 g) uncooked bacon, diced into ½-inch (1 cm) pieces

¼ cup (60 mL) extra virgin olive oil

2 sweet onions, peeled and diced into ½-inch (1.25 cm) cubes

½ tsp (2.5 mL) sea salt

½ cup (125 mL) light brown sugar

¼ cup (60 mL) honey

1 tsp (5 mL) cayenne pepper

½ tsp (2.5 mL) ground black pepper

½ tsp (2.5 mL) fresh chopped thyme

1 tsp (5 mL) fresh chopped rosemary

Zest of 1 orange

¼ cup (60 mL) raspberry vinegar

1 cup (250 mL) bourbon

BBQ BOURBON EDAMAME

{ MAKES 4 SERVINGS }

Charred and slightly smoked with a hint of spices, the sweetness of the barbecue sauce and bourbon rounds out the flavour to make these protein-packed vegetables irresistible.

INGREDIENTS

One 10 oz (283 g) pkg frozen edamame

2 Tbsp (30 mL) extra virgin olive oil

1 Tbsp (15 mL) sesame seed oil

3 Tbsp (45 mL) barbecue sauce

2 Tbsp (30 mL) bourbon

2 tsp (10 mL) sweet chili sauce

¼ tsp (1 mL) soy sauce

1 tsp (5 mL) sea salt

2 tsp (10 mL) sesame seeds

2 Tbsp (30 mL) cilantro

INSTRUCTIONS In a medium saucepan, add water and bring to a boil over medium heat. Add the frozen edamame and boil for 1 minute. Strain the water through a colander and briefly set the edamame aside.

In a large bowl, stir together olive oil, sesame seed oil, barbecue sauce, bourbon, sweet chili sauce and soy sauce. Toss the warm edamame in the bowl and let it marinate in the glaze for 15 minutes.

Heat a large pan over medium heat. Add the glazed edamame and cook quickly, for about 3 minutes, until the sides start to char. Place the edamame in a bowl and sprinkle with the salt, sesame seeds and cilantro. Serve while hot.

SOUTHERN BANANAS FOSTER

{ MAKES 4 SERVINGS }

This reworked version of Bananas Foster is a play on the flavours of a peanut butter and jelly sandwich. It's both whimsical and yummy. It's also versatile—I use it on top of vanilla ice cream, pancakes and French toast!

INSTRUCTIONS In a large skillet, melt the butter over medium heat. Stir in the brown sugar, orange zest and bourbon. Once the mixture starts to boil, reduce heat to low, add the banana halves and continue cooking for 3 minutes. Add the chopped peanuts and continue cooking until the bananas are slightly soft, about 1 more minute.

In a small bowl, mash together the raspberries and granulated sugar.

With a large spoon, remove the bananas from the skillet and place on top of your favourite vanilla ice cream, pancakes or French toast. Drizzle the warm peanut caramel bourbon sauce overtop, then finish with a dollop of mashed raspberries on top.

INGREDIENTS

¼ cup (60 mL) unsalted butter

½ cup (125 mL) light brown sugar

Zest of 1 orange

¼ cup (60 mL) bourbon

4 bananas, peeled and cut lengthwise into halves

¼ cup (60 mL) coarsely chopped roasted salted peanuts

2 cups (500 mL) fresh raspberries

½ cup (125 mL) granulated sugar

Vanilla ice cream for serving (optional)

WARM PEACH AND BOURBON COBBLER

{ MAKES 8 SERVINGS }

When you bake with peaches, you know you are well into summer's barbecue season. That means spending leisurely time with family and friends. Put this cobbler on the menu to inspire some sweet baking memories—hopefully the generous addition of bourbon won't turn these into fuzzy memories.

PEACH FILLING

6 fresh peaches

¾ cup (180 mL) light brown sugar

¼ cup (60 mL) granulated sugar

½ tsp (2.5 mL) ground cinnamon

1 tsp (5 mL) vanilla extract

½ cup (125 mL) bourbon

¼ tsp (1 mL) sea salt

TOPPING

½ cup (125 mL) unsalted butter

1 cup (250 mL) whole wheat flour

1 cup (250 mL) all-purpose flour

½ cup (125 mL) granulated sugar

½ cup (125 mL) light brown sugar

2 tsp (10 mL) baking powder

½ tsp (2.5 mL) grated orange zest

1¼ cups (310 mL) buttermilk

1 large egg

¼ cup (60 mL) icing sugar

Ice cream for serving

INSTRUCTIONS FOR PEACH FILLING Remove the pit from each peach then slice into 6 wedges. In a large bowl, add the peach wedges and combine with the sugars, cinnamon, vanilla extract, bourbon and salt. Transfer the mixture to a lightly greased cast iron pan.

INSTRUCTIONS FOR TOPPING In a small saucepan, melt the butter over low heat.

In a medium bowl, stir together both flours and sugars with the baking powder and orange zest.

In another medium bowl, whisk together the buttermilk, egg and melted butter. Stir the wet ingredients into flour mixture, then pour the batter evenly over the filling.

ASSEMBLY Preheat oven to 360°F (180°C).

Place the cast iron pan on a baking tray and bake for 45 minutes, until the top is a light golden colour.

Remove the baking tray from the oven and place on a cooling rack. While still hot, dust the top of the cobbler with icing sugar.

Serve warm with a scoop of your favourite ice cream on top.

STICKY TOFFEE BOURBON PUDDING

{ MAKES 4 SINGLE-SERVING CAKES }

It might be called a pudding, but sticky toffee pudding is actually more like a cake. This is the same iconic dessert that British expats yearn for when they're away from home, but the cheeky addition of bourbon lends it a distinctly North American accent. It is equally as enticing as the traditional version.

BOURBON TOFFEE SAUCE

1 vanilla bean, split open

¼ cup (60 mL) cold unsalted butter

1½ cups (375 mL) whole milk

½ cup (125 mL) granulated sugar

½ cup (125 mL) light brown sugar

¼ cup (60 mL) honey

¾ cup (180 mL) bourbon

½ cup (125 mL) whipping cream

½ tsp (2.5 mL) instant coffee

CAKE

1 cup (250 mL) chopped dried figs

½ cup (125 mL) water

¼ cup (60 mL) bourbon

¼ cup (60 mL) canola oil

½ cup (125 mL) granulated sugar

1 large egg

1 cup (250 mL) all-purpose flour

1 tsp (5 mL) baking powder

¼ tsp (1 mL) baking soda

¼ tsp (1 mL) sea salt

¼ tsp (1 mL) ground cinnamon

Unsweetened whipped cream or ice cream for serving (optional)

INSTRUCTIONS FOR BOURBON TOFFEE SAUCE In a medium saucepan, combine the butter, milk and both sugars. Bring to a boil over medium heat and cook for 5 minutes.

Remove saucepan from heat and add the honey, bourbon and vanilla bean. Return to the stove and cook over low heat, stirring frequently, for 6 minutes, until the mixture turns into a light golden caramel.

Remove saucepan from heat and, using a small hand whisk, pour in the whipping cream. Be careful of the hot steam in the saucepan. Stir in the instant coffee.

Strain the sauce through a fine mesh sieve into a medium bowl. Set aside to cool at room temperature until needed.

INSTRUCTIONS FOR CAKE Preheat oven to 360°F (180°C).

In a small saucepan, cook the figs, water and bourbon over low heat. Use a wooden spoon to stir occasionally, until the liquid is absorbed. Set aside until needed.

In an electric mixing bowl with the whisk attachment, blend the canola oil and sugar on medium speed for 1 minute. Add the egg and whisk for about 5 minutes on medium speed.

In a small bowl, stir together all the remaining ingredients. Add to the oil mixture, mixing on low speed for 2 minutes. Add the cooked figs and mix until fully incorporated.

Grease and flour the 4 ramekins. Pour the cake batter up to the top of each ramekin, then place ramekins on a baking tray. Bake for about 30 minutes. Once baked, the tip of a knife or a toothpick inserted into the centre of the cake should come out clean.

Remove the baking tray from the oven and place on a wire rack to cool.

ASSEMBLY Once fully cooled, remove cakes from the ramekins and slice each cake in half horizontally using a serrated knife. Place one half in a bowl-like plate and spoon a generous amount of bourbon toffee sauce overtop. Place the other half on top with more sauce. Repeat with the remaining cakes.

Top each sticky toffee pudding with a generous amount of unsweetened whipped cream or, if you are a traditionalist, ice cream.

BOURBON "OLD FASHIONED" BUTTERSCOTCH PUDDING

{ MAKES 6 CUSTARDS }

Cocktails can be a great inspiration when trying to come up with a new dessert. Bartenders are wizards, and this recipe demonstrates how well the flavour combinations they use to make their magical concoctions lend themselves to the culinary world. This playful, easy-to-make dessert is based on a classic old fashioned cocktail.

INGREDIENTS

¼ cup (60 mL) unsalted butter

¾ cup (180 mL) light brown sugar

2½ cups (625 mL) whipping cream

1 cup (250 mL) whole milk

3 Tbsp (45 mL) bourbon

2 large eggs

6 egg yolks

¼ cup (60 mL) granulated sugar

¼ cup (60 mL) cornstarch

Zest of 1 orange

2 tsp (10 mL) Angostura bitters

Whipped cream or chocolate sauce for serving (optional)

INSTRUCTIONS In a medium saucepan, melt the butter over low heat and cook until it starts to brown and produces a nutty scent. With a wooden spoon, stir in the brown sugar and cook for another 2 minutes. Add the whipping cream, milk and bourbon and bring to a quick simmer. Remove from heat and set aside at room temperature.

In a medium bowl, mix the eggs, yolks, granulated sugar and cornstarch with a hand whisk until the mixture turns a pale yellow colour. Gradually whisk in the warm butter mixture until both parts are completely incorporated.

Pour the mixture back into the saucepan and place over medium heat. Stir continuously and cook until a custard forms, about 5 minutes.

Pass the custard through a fine mesh sieve into a medium bowl to remove any sugar or egg yolk lumps. Add the orange zest and bitters and pour an equal amount of custard into the 6 ramequins. Refrigerate for 2 hours before serving.

The pudding can be made up to 2 days ahead. Once chilled, wrap the custards individually in plastic wrap. They are great with a dollop of whipped cream and a drizzle of chocolate sauce.

BOURBON AND PUMPKIN COFFEE CAKE WITH TOASTED CINNAMON MERINGUE FROSTING

{ MAKES ONE 8-INCH (20 CM) CAKE }

There is something magical about this rustic-yet-elegant cake. Moist and flavourful, it conjures up memories of family gatherings. It's perfect for any occasion across the seasons: birthday party, summer barbecue or holiday gathering.

BOURBON AND PUMPKIN COFFEE CAKE BATTER

1½ cups (375 mL) light brown sugar

1 cup (250 mL) softened unsalted butter

3 large eggs

2 egg yolks (reserve the whites for the cinnamon meringue)

3 cups (750 mL) cake flour

1 tsp (5 mL) baking soda

½ tsp (2.5 mL) baking powder

½ tsp (2.5 mL) sea salt

1 tsp (5 mL) ground cinnamon

2 Tbsp (30 mL) instant coffee

½ cup (125 mL) bourbon

1 cup (250 mL) sour cream

¾ cup (180 mL) canned pumpkin purée

TOASTED CINNAMON MERINGUE FROSTING

2 egg whites

¼ cup (60 mL) granulated sugar

3 Tbsp (45 mL) icing sugar

1 tsp (5 mL) ground cinnamon

INSTRUCTIONS FOR BOURBON AND PUMPKIN COFFEE CAKE BATTER Preheat oven to 360°F (180°C).

In an electric mixing bowl with the paddle attachment, beat together the sugar and butter on medium speed until creamy and light. Use a rubber spatula to scrape down the sides of the bowl.

Reduce speed to low and beat in the eggs and yolks until combined.

In a medium bowl, stir together the flour, baking soda, baking powder, salt, cinnamon and instant coffee. Add the flour mixture to the creamed butter, sugar and eggs and mix on low speed until blended. Add the bourbon, sour cream and pumpkin purée and continue mixing on low for 1 minute, until the cake batter is well combined. Remember to stop the mixing frequently to scrape down the sides of the bowl.

Grease the inside of an 8-inch (20 cm) springform cake pan. Pour the batter into the pan and bake for 40 minutes. Once baked, the tip of a knife or a toothpick inserted into the centre of the cake should come out clean.

Remove cake from the oven and place on a cooling rack. Unmould once cooled. The cake can be made a day ahead, wrapped in plastic and refrigerated.

INSTRUCTIONS FOR TOASTED CINNAMON MERINGUE FROSTING In an electric mixing bowl with the whisk attachment, beat the egg whites on medium speed. Once the egg whites start to foam, gradually add the granulated sugar until fully incorporated, then increase to full speed and whisk until soft peaks form.

Remove the bowl from the electric mixer. Combine the icing sugar and ground cinnamon in a small bowl then gently fold into the whipped egg whites.

ASSEMBLY Place the cake on a serving plate and, using an offset spatula, spread the cinnamon meringue all over the top. Using a small propane torch, toast the top of the meringue into a light brown colour.

WHITE CAKE WITH BOURBON BUTTERCREAM

{ MAKES ONE 8-INCH (20 CM) CAKE }

A simple white cake, depending on its filling and finish, can suit any occasion—from a casual barbecue to an elegant formal birthday dinner. For this recipe, the bourbon buttercream frosting gives the cake a decidedly sassy yet sophisticated flavour kick.

WHITE CAKE BATTER

1 cup (250 mL) granulated sugar

¾ cup (180 mL) softened unsalted butter

1 tsp (5 mL) vanilla extract

2 large eggs

1 egg yolk

1½ cups (375 mL) all-purpose flour

½ tsp (2.5 mL) baking soda

1 tsp (5 mL) baking powder

½ cup (125 mL) sour cream

¼ cup (60 mL) buttermilk

BOURBON BUTTERCREAM

1 cup (250 mL) softened unsalted butter

2 cups (500 mL) icing sugar

3 Tbsp (45 mL) whole milk

¼ cup (60 mL) bourbon

2 tsp (10 mL) vanilla extract

Zest of 1 orange

INSTRUCTIONS FOR WHITE CAKE BATTER Preheat oven to 360°F (180°C).

In an electric mixing bowl with the paddle attachment, beat together the sugar and butter on medium speed until creamy and light. Add the vanilla extract. Use a rubber spatula to scrape down the sides of the bowl. Reduce speed to low and beat in the eggs and yolk, followed by the flour, baking soda and baking powder until combined. Finally, add the sour cream and buttermilk. Beat on low speed for 1 minute to be sure the cake batter is well combined.

Grease the inside of an 8-inch (20 cm) springform cake pan. Pour the batter into the pan and bake for 30 minutes. Once baked, the tip of a knife or a toothpick inserted into the centre of the cake should come out clean.

Remove cake from the oven and let it cool on a wire rack. Unmould once cooled.

The cake can be made a day ahead, wrapped in plastic and refrigerated.

INSTRUCTIONS FOR BOURBON BUTTERCREAM In an electric mixing bowl with the whisk attachment, beat the butter on medium speed until light and creamy. Reduce speed to low and add the icing sugar until the mixture is smooth. Scrape down the sides of the bowl with a rubber spatula to ensure there are no lumps. Gradually increase the speed to medium, then add the milk, bourbon, vanilla extract and orange zest. Beat for another 2 minutes on medium speed until smooth.

Transfer the buttercream to a container, cover with plastic wrap and set aside at room temperature until needed.

ASSEMBLY Place the cake on a turntable. Use the palm of your hand on top of the cake to hold it in place; with your other hand, use a long serrated bread knife to slice the cake horizontally into 3 layers. Place the 2 top layers on the side.

Using a metal spatula, spread the bourbon buttercream about ½ inch (1 cm) thick overtop the bottom cake layer. Place the second layer on top and add more buttercream. Finally, place the third layer on top and refrigerate the whole cake for 20 minutes until the buttercream sets.

Remove cake from the fridge and, using a spatula, cover the entire cake with the remaining bourbon buttercream. Place the cake on a platter and refrigerate for at least 30 minutes before serving.

APPLE WALNUT BOURBON CAKE WITH CHOCOLATE BOURBON GLAZE

{ MAKES ONE 8-INCH (20 CM) CAKE }

The tart acidic flavour of green apple is beautifully balanced by the sweet aroma of bourbon, and tossing in the walnuts and cranberries brings additional crunch and flavour dimensions. This recipe is one of my favourite cakes to make around the holidays. Topping it with a chocolate bourbon glaze makes it a favourite of everyone.

APPLE WALNUT BOURBON CAKE BATTER

2 cups (500 mL) peeled, cored and diced green apples

½ cup (125 mL) dried cranberries

½ cup (125 mL) granulated sugar

½ cup (125 mL) bourbon

1½ cups (375 mL) light brown sugar

1 cup (250 mL) softened unsalted butter

4 large eggs

1 tsp (5 mL) vanilla extract

2 cups (500 mL) all-purpose flour

1 tsp (5 mL) baking powder

¾ cup (180 mL) chopped walnuts

1 tsp (5 mL) ground cinnamon

½ tsp (2.5 mL) sea salt

¾ cup (180 mL) buttermilk

CHOCOLATE BOURBON GLAZE

1 cup (250 mL) whole milk

½ cup (125 mL) bourbon

¼ cup (60 mL) granulated sugar

¼ cup (60 mL) light corn syrup

¼ cup (60 mL) softened unsalted butter

1 cup (250 mL) chopped extra bitter chocolate

INSTRUCTIONS FOR APPLE WALNUT BOURBON CAKE BATTER Preheat oven to 350°F (175°C).

In a large saucepan, cook the diced apples, dried cranberries and granulated sugar over medium heat, stirring occasionally with a wooden spoon. After 5 minutes, add the bourbon and cook for another 8 minutes. Remove from heat and set aside at room temperature.

In an electric mixing bowl with the paddle attachment, beat together the brown sugar and butter on medium speed until creamy and light. Use a rubber spatula to scrape down the sides of the bowl. Reduce speed to low, beat in the eggs and mix until fully incorporated.

In a separate large bowl, stir together the flour, baking powder, walnuts, cinnamon, salt and baking powder. Add the dry mixture to the butter mixture and beat on low speed. Add the buttermilk and apple mixture, including the cooking juices, and mix on low speed for 1 minute to ensure the batter is well combined.

Grease the inside of an 8-inch (20 cm) springform cake pan. Pour the batter into the pan and bake for 45 minutes, until the top is golden brown. Once baked, the tip of a knife or a toothpick inserted into the centre of the cake should come out clean.

Remove cake from the oven and place on a cooling rack. Unmould once cooled. The cake can be made a day ahead, wrapped in plastic and refrigerated.

INSTRUCTIONS FOR CHOCOLATE BOURBON GLAZE In a medium saucepan, bring the milk, bourbon, sugar and corn syrup to a boil over medium heat. Remove from heat and whisk in the butter and chocolate until completely melted and incorporated.

Pass the chocolate glaze through a fine mesh sieve. While still lukewarm, pour the glaze over of the cake and serve.

BOURBON VANILLA CANNED PINEAPPLE

{ MAKES SIX 2-CUP (500 ML) JARS }

Your pantry should be full of homemade canned fruits. Canning is such a classic and—even more important—sustainable way to process locally sourced seasonal fruits. I know I might be contradicting myself a bit here by using pineapple but, hey, I wrote this recipe from the shores of Maui! Canned fruits are delicious on their own, or used as a topping for cakes, ice creams, salads or even roasted meats or fish.

INGREDIENTS

6 Mason jars with unfastened lids and rings

1 golden pineapple (fully ripened)

2 cups (500 mL) bourbon

1 cup (250 mL) granulated sugar

2 cups (500 mL) canned pineapple juice

3 vanilla beans, split open

6 cardamom pods

½ cup (125 mL) light brown sugar

INSTRUCTIONS Fill a large pot three-quarters full with water and bring to a boil over high heat. Submerge the jars, lids and rings for 10 minutes.

Remove pot from heat and let it rest for 30 minutes at room temperature. Using large tongs, remove everything from the pot and place on a clean kitchen towel.

Using a large knife, cut the top off the pineapple and remove the skin. Cut the flesh into quarters and remove the hard core. Cut each quarter in half, then halve again for pieces small enough to fit into the Mason jars.

In a medium saucepan, bring the bourbon, granulated sugar and pineapple juice to a quick boil over medium heat. Remove from heat. Scrape the seeds inside the vanilla beans and add both the pods and seeds to the syrup while stirring.

Place a cardamom pod in each jar. Remove vanilla pods from the hot liquid and place one piece inside each jar. Pour or ladle the hot bourbon mixture into the jars until half-filled. Pack each jar with chunks of pineapple then fill them to their tops with the rest of the liquid.

Using a clean towel to wipe the rim of each jar clean, place a lid on top of each jar then twist on the ring cap. Flip each jar upside down to make sure it is completely closed. Return jars to the large pot of water so that they're submerged and return pot to the heat. Bring to a boil for 20 minutes, adding more water if necessary (the jars need to remain completely covered in water during the boiling process).

Remove pot from the stove and let it cool, then remove jars from the water and place on a dry clean towel. Let the jars cool at room temperature for 6 hours.

Write the date of canning on each jar and store in a cool dark pantry. Jars should be stored for a full month for the optimum flavour to develop. Once opened, they should be refrigerated and used within 4 days.

BOURBON PANNA COTTA WITH ORANGE MARMALADE

{ MAKES 6 SERVINGS }

These are two very simple recipes, but when served together they create magic in your mouth. The creaminess of the delicate panna cotta and the slightly bitter and sweet orange marmalade are pure bliss.

PANNA COTTA

1½ cups (375 mL) whipping cream

½ cup (125 mL) whole milk

½ cup (125 mL) granulated sugar

1 tsp (5 mL) vanilla extract

2 Tbsp (30 mL) honey

3 Tbsp (45 mL) cold water

1 packet unflavoured gelatin

5 Tbsp (75 mL) bourbon

ORANGE MARMALADE

3 medium oranges

2 cups (500 mL) water

3½ cups (875 mL) granulated sugar

¼ cup (60 mL) bourbon

INSTRUCTIONS FOR PANNA COTTA In a medium saucepan, heat the whipping cream, milk, sugar, vanilla extract and honey over medium heat until simmering. Remove from heat and set aside.

In a small bowl, add the cold water. Sprinkle the gelatin into the water then stir with a fork to allow the gelatin to bloom (absorb the liquid). Whisk the bloomed gelatin into the milk mixture, then add the bourbon. Stir well.

Pour an equal amount of the still-warm panna cotta into six 1-cup (250 mL) jars or ramequins. Place the jars on a tray and refrigerate for 2 hours. This recipe can be made up to 2 days ahead.

INSTRUCTIONS FOR ORANGE MARMALADE Wash the oranges under warm water, then slice them into ⅛-inch (3 mm) rounds with a large knife, removing any seeds.

In a medium saucepan, add the water and whisk in the sugar. Place over medium heat and bring to a quick boil. Remove from heat and add the sliced oranges and bourbon.

Return saucepan to the stove and bring to a simmer over low heat, stirring with a wooden spoon every so often. Cook for about 25 minutes until the orange skin is soft, then remove from heat and allow to cool at room temperature. Place in an airtight container and refrigerate until needed.

ASSEMBLY Spoon about ⅓ cup (80 mL) of the orange marmalade on top of each portion of panna cotta and serve.

BOURBON "TRÉS" TRES LECHES CAKE

{ MAKES 8 SERVINGS }

Here's a new spin—and a play on words—for this delicious tres leches cake recipe. I include the French word "très" (meaning "very") because, for it to be great, a tres leches cake has to soak up the sweet leche (milk) like a sponge, then let its excess creaminess escape out the sides.

CAKE BATTER

½ cup (125 mL) softened unsalted butter

½ cup (125 mL) granulated sugar

½ cup (125 mL) light brown sugar

4 large eggs

1¼ cups (310 mL) all-purpose flour

¼ cup (60 mL) semolina

¼ tsp (1 mL) sea salt

1 tsp (5 mL) baking powder

Zest of 1 lemon

TRES LECHES SOAK

1 vanilla bean

1 cup (250 mL) whole milk

1 cup (250 mL) condensed milk

1 cup (250 mL) evaporated milk

1 cup (250 mL) bourbon

½ cup (125 mL) granulated sugar

Whipped cream for serving

Fresh raspberries for serving

INSTRUCTIONS FOR CAKE BATTER Preheat oven to 350°F (175°C).

In an electric mixing bowl with the paddle attachment, cream together the butter and both sugars on medium-low speed. Use a rubber spatula to scrape down the sides of the bowl and ensure a smooth mix. Add the eggs one by one while mixing at low speed, stopping from time to time to scrape down the sides of the bowl, then increase speed to medium and mix for another 3 minutes. Be sure all ingredients are fully incorporated and the batter is free of lumps.

In a large bowl, stir together the flour, semolina, salt, baking powder and lemon zest. Beat the flour mixture into the butter mixture on low speed.

Grease a 9-inch (23 cm) springform cake pan. Pour the batter into the pan and bake for 30 minutes. When done, transfer to a cooling rack until cooled completely.

Once cool, wrap the cake in plastic and refrigerate for 3 hours. The cake can be made the day before and kept refrigerated.

INSTRUCTIONS FOR TRES LECHES SOAK Using a small knife, split the vanilla bean lengthwise and scrape the seeds into a medium saucepan along with all three types of milk and the bourbon. Place over medium heat until it starts to simmer; simmer for 1 minute then remove from heat. Allow the saucepan to cool at room temperature for 1 hour then refrigerate, uncovered, for 2 more hours before using.

ASSEMBLY Place the cake on a deep-dish platter. Using a small knife or bamboo skewers, poke the cake 20 times so that the liquid can soak in. Using a ladle, slowly pour the cold tres leches liquid over the top of the cake, letting it slowly absorb the liquid like a sponge. Top with whipped cream and fresh raspberries.

chapter 4

CHOCOLATE

CHOCOLATE

WE OFTEN FORGET that chocolate at its core is a fermented product. The cocoa beans are fermented before being roasted and crushed into a paste, then processed into chocolate after adding cocoa butter, sugar and often vanilla.

Because the fermentation helps develop the flavours, picking a chocolate high in cocoa solids and low in sugar is important. Too much sugar, and the flavours are flat and the overall finish in the mouth is just sweetness.

Sugary chocolate is easier to work with when whipping into a mousse or ganache, as the sugar helps with fluidity and elasticity, but its flavour can lack depth. Chocolates with a higher cocoa solid percentage (such as those labeled 65% and higher) have much deeper, richer and more refined flavours, but are sometimes difficult to work with, lacking fluidity and texture. Finding the right balance can be frustrating.

Although not an outright endorsement, I enjoy working with the chocolate brand Callebaut, which is great for managing technical concerns while building great baking skills. It is a good stable chocolate overall with nice clean flavours, and it's easy to find and bake with.

COCOA AND MOLASSES BABY BACK RIBS

{ MAKES 6 SERVINGS }

These fingers-licking baby back ribs are the perfect casual meal that's easy to prepare and cook. Warm chocolate flavours blend with the fat from the ribs in a magical way, creating some amazing flavours that pop in your mouth.

INGREDIENTS

½ cup (125 mL) unsweetened cocoa powder

½ cup (125 mL) light brown sugar

1 Tbsp (15 mL) kosher salt

2 Tbsp (30 mL) light soy sauce

½ cup (125 mL) light molasses

¼ cup (60 mL) rice vinegar

½ cup (125 mL) extra virgin olive oil + extra for the roasting pan

1 tsp (5 mL) fresh chopped thyme

1 Tbsp (15 mL) fresh grated ginger

1 Tbsp (15 mL) fresh chopped garlic

1 tsp (5 mL) fresh ground black pepper

Zest of 1 orange

3 lb (1.3 kg) baby back pork ribs

2 medium yellow onions

INSTRUCTIONS In a large bowl, whisk together all the ingredients except the ribs and onions.

Line a baking tray with plastic wrap and place the baby back ribs in the middle. Rub the baby back ribs all over with the cocoa marinade. Wrap the ribs in plastic and marinate for 12 hours in the refrigerator.

Preheat oven to 360°F (180°C).

Peel and slice the onions into ¼-inch (0.5 cm) rings and place them in an olive oil–drizzled roasting pan. Unwrap the marinated ribs and place them on top of the onions. Drizzle any excess cocoa marinade on top of the ribs.

Cover the entire tray with aluminium foil and bake for 50 minutes, until the ribs are tender. Remove ribs from the oven and increase the oven temperature to 420°F (220°C). Return ribs to the oven and bake for another 10 minutes.

Serve ribs on a platter alongside your favourite roasted vegetables. Enjoy!

DOUBLE CHOCOLATE WHOOPIE PIES

{ MAKES 12 WHOOPIE PIES }

If you find the idea of making macarons too intimidating, then whoopie pies are definitely a good alternative in the sweet "sandwich" world. You can be very creative with flavours, and they make perfect little gifts for any occasion. Coffee and cardamom create a small flavour boost in this recipe, but the overall taste is all about chocolate.

CHOCOLATE DOUGH

½ cup (125 mL) softened unsalted butter

½ cup (125 mL) granulated sugar

½ cup (125 mL) light brown sugar

3 egg yolks

2 cups (500 mL) all-purpose flour

6 Tbsp (90 mL) cocoa powder

½ tsp (2.5 mL) sea salt

1 tsp (5 mL) baking soda

1 tsp (5 mL) baking powder

¼ tsp (1 mL) ground cardamom

1 cup (250 mL) buttermilk

¼ cup (60 mL) icing sugar

CHOCOLATE FILLING

1 cup (250 mL) softened unsalted butter

1¾ cups (430 mL) icing sugar

½ cup (125 mL) cocoa powder

1 tsp (5 mL) instant coffee

INSTRUCTIONS FOR CHOCOLATE DOUGH Preheat oven to 360°F (180°C).

In an electric mixing bowl with the paddle attachment, cream together the butter and both sugars at medium speed. Use a rubber spatula to scrape down the sides of the bowl. Add the egg yolks and continue mixing on medium speed until fully incorporated.

In a medium bowl, stir together the flour, cocoa powder, salt, baking soda, baking powder and ground cardamom. Add the flour mixture to the butter mixture a bit at a time, alternating with the buttermilk while mixing at low speed. Mix for another 5 minutes on medium speed until the batter has a nice soft texture.

Using a soup spoon, drop egg yolk–size spoonfuls of batter onto a parchment-lined baking tray, spacing the spoonfuls 3 inches (8 cm) apart from each other. Using a small sieve, dust each batter ball with icing sugar.

Bake for 12 minutes, then remove from the oven and place on a cooling rack.

INSTRUCTIONS FOR CHOCOLATE FILLING In an electric mixing bowl with the whisk attachment, whip the butter with the sugar on medium speed for 5 minutes until the mixture is fluffy. Scrape down the sides of the bowl.

Add the cocoa powder and instant coffee and mix until combined.

ASSEMBLY Spread a good amount of chocolate buttercream on top of a baked cookie then top with another cookie to create a "sandwich." Repeat with the remaining cookies.

Store the whoopie pies in an airtight container in a cool dry place—although it's unlikely these delicious cookies will last long..

CHOCOLATE ESPRESSO ÉCLAIRS

{ MAKES 6 LARGE ÉCLAIRS }

It is truly a sensory experience to bite into an éclair, have the pastry cream ooze out and then have to lick it off your fingers. I like to use equal amounts of water and milk for the choux paste, as it creates a perfect balance between texture and flavour. Some recipes use only water, but I find the choux lacking. Other recipes use only milk, which I find results in a texture that's too heavy.

CHOCOLATE PASTRY CREAM

6 egg yolks

½ cup (125 mL) granulated sugar

¼ cup (60 mL) cornstarch

2 cups (500 mL) whole milk

2 Tbsp (30 mL) cocoa powder

ESPRESSO CHOUX PASTE

½ cup (125 mL) water

½ cup (125 mL) whole milk

¼ tsp (1 mL) sea salt

½ cup (125 mL) cold unsalted butter, cut into ¼-inch (1 cm) cubes

1 cup (250 mL) all-purpose flour

4 large eggs + 1 egg for egg wash

2 Tbsp (30 mL) instant coffee

½ cup (125 mL) chopped bittersweet chocolate

INSTRUCTIONS FOR CHOCOLATE PASTRY CREAM In a small bowl, whisk together the egg yolks, sugar and cornstarch until the mixture turns pale yellow.

In a medium saucepan, bring the milk to a quick boil. Pour the milk over the egg mixture, stirring well. Pour everything back into the saucepan and bring to a boil while constantly stirring with a hand whisk.

Once the cream starts to boil, remove from heat and pass the cream through a fine mesh sieve into a container. Stir in the cocoa powder. Cover the pastry cream with a plastic film, applied directly to the surface to avoid creating a skin. Refrigerate for 4 hours before using.

Pastry cream can be kept refrigerated up to 5 days.

INSTRUCTIONS FOR ESPRESSO CHOUX PASTE In a medium saucepan, bring the water, milk, salt and cubed butter to a boil. Remove from heat and stir in the flour with a wooden spatula until the mixture comes together.

Return saucepan to the stove and cook the paste for another 2 minutes over low heat while continuously stirring.

Transfer the cooked choux paste to an electric mixing bowl with the paddle attachment. Mix on medium speed to allow the mixture to cool slowly.

In a small bowl, beat the eggs by hand for 30 seconds, then slowly add the paste mixture while mixing at low speed. Scrape down the sides of the bowl to ensure the choux dough is mixed properly. Add the instant coffee and mix for another 4 minutes on medium speed. Remove the bowl and cover the top with a dry towel.

. . . recipe continued

Fit a large piping bag with a 1-inch (2.5 cm) round tip. Fill the piping bag with half the choux dough and pipe the dough onto a parchment-lined baking tray in 5-inch-long (12 cm) lines, spacing each line 2 inches (5 cm) apart from each other. Place the tray in the freezer for 30 minutes.

Preheat oven to 420°F (220°C).

In a small bowl, beat the remaining egg for the egg wash. Remove tray from the freezer and brush egg wash along the entire length of each éclair, including the sides. Place the tray in the oven and bake for about 25 minutes. The éclairs will puff and bake into a light golden colour.

Remove tray from the oven and place on a cooling rack. If desired, you can freeze the unfilled éclairs for a few days by storing them in an airtight container.

ASSEMBLY Place a double boiler over medium heat. Add the bittersweet chocolate to the bowl, and allow it to melt slowly. Keep warm until needed.

Pour the pastry cream into a medium bowl and beat it until smooth using a hand whisk. Fit a piping bag with a small tip and fill it with the chocolate pastry cream. Poke a hole at both ends of each éclair, then pipe pastry cream into the holes until the éclairs start to feel heavy (70 percent of the éclair's weight should be pastry cream).

Place éclairs on a tray. Drizzle with some melted dark chocolate.

LEMON RICOTTA CHOCOLATE CHEESECAKE

{ MAKES ONE 9-INCH (23 CM) CHEESECAKE }

This cheesecake would be at home in the window of an Italian bakery. The original recipe was just flavoured with lemon, but combining it with dark chocolate adds an extra dimension to the fresh citrus taste.

CRUST

1 cup (250 mL) ground graham crackers

½ cup (125 mL) ground hazelnuts

½ cup (125 mL) light brown sugar

¼ cup (60 mL) melted unsalted butter

FILLING

1 cup (250 mL) softened cream cheese

1¼ cups (310 mL) granulated sugar

3 large eggs

2 cups (500 mL) whipping cream

¼ tsp (1 mL) sea salt

¼ cup (60 mL) cornstarch

3 tsp (15 mL) fresh grated lemon zest

2 cups (500 mL) ricotta cheese

¾ cup (180 mL) chopped extra bitter chocolate

INSTRUCTIONS FOR CRUST Preheat oven to 325°F (150°C). Cut a round piece of parchment paper to fit evenly at the bottom of a 9-inch (23 cm) nonstick springform pan.

In a small bowl, stir together the graham crackers, hazelnuts, sugar and melted butter. Press the mixture down evenly on the bottom of a 9-inch (23 cm) nonstick springform pan fitted with the round parchment paper.

Bake for 10 minutes, until the crust is light golden in colour. Remove from the oven and set aside at room temperature, but maintain the oven temperature.

INSTRUCTIONS FOR FILLING In an electric mixing bowl with the paddle attachment, cream together the cream cheese and sugar at low speed. Add the eggs and continue mixing for 2 minutes. Scrape down the sides of the bowl using a rubber spatula to ensure the mixture is smooth and free of cream cheese lumps. Add the whipping cream, salt, cornstarch and lemon zest and mix until well combined. Remove the bowl from the mixer and fold in the ricotta cheese.

ASSEMBLY Pour half of the cheesecake filling into the springform pan. Sprinkle the chopped chocolate evenly overtop, then add the remaining filling.

Bake in the preheated oven for about 60 minutes, until the edges of the cheesecake are light golden in colour and the centre is firm-ish. Remove from the oven and rest on a cooling rack for 1 hour, then place in the refrigerator for 3 hours before serving.

TRIPLE CHOCOLATE, BACON AND SOUR CREAM CAKE

{ MAKES ONE 9-INCH (23 CM) CAKE }

Sour cream is the magic ingredient that makes this cake perfectly moist. Anytime I find a cake recipe too dry for my liking, I adjust it by adding sour cream. It's always an easy fix.

CAKE BATTER

1 cup (250 mL) softened unsalted butter

1 cup (250 mL) granulated sugar

½ cup (125 mL) light brown sugar

½ tsp (2.5 mL) sea salt

⅓ cup (80 mL) cocoa powder

1½ tsp (7.5 mL) baking soda

1 tsp (5 mL) baking powder

¼ cup (60 mL) honey

3 large eggs

2 cups (500 mL) all-purpose flour

¾ cup (180 mL) whole milk

¾ cup (180 mL) sour cream

½ cup (125 mL) chopped milk chocolate

½ cup (125 mL) chopped white chocolate

CHOCOLATE BACON GLAZE

¼ cup (60 mL) whole milk

¼ cup (60 mL) whipping cream

1 Tbsp (15 mL) honey

1 Tbsp (15 mL) light corn syrup

2 Tbsp (30 mL) granulated sugar

½ cup (125 mL) chopped extra bitter chocolate

¼ cup (60 mL) crispy bacon bits, divided (see page 13)

INSTRUCTIONS FOR CAKE BATTER Preheat oven to 360°F (180°C).

Cut a round piece of parchment paper to fit evenly at the bottom of a 9-inch (23 cm) nonstick springform pan. Cut two 3½ × 15 inch (9 × 38 cm) strips of parchment paper and place them (overlapping) on the inner sides of the pan.

In an electric mixing bowl with the paddle attachment, cream together the butter and both sugars on medium speed. Scrape down the sides of the bowl using a plastic spatula. Add the salt, cocoa powder, baking soda and baking powder. Once fully incorporated, add the honey and eggs. Scrape down the sides of the bowl to ensure the batter is smooth and free of lumps.

Reduce speed to low and add half the flour, milk, sour cream and, lastly, the other half of the flour. Continue mixing until the batter is smooth. Remove the bowl from the mixer stand and, using a rubber spatula, stir in the chopped milk chocolate and white chocolate by hand.

Pour the batter into the prepared pan and bake in the oven for about 40 minutes. Once baked, the tip of a knife or a toothpick inserted into the centre of the cake should come out clean.

Remove cake from the oven and allow it to cool for 15 minutes on a cooling rack. While the cake is cooling, make the chocolate bacon glaze.

INSTRUCTIONS FOR CHOCOLATE BACON GLAZE In a small saucepan, bring the milk, whipping cream, honey, corn syrup and sugar to a boil. Remove from heat and, while still hot, whisk in the chopped chocolate. Stir until the chocolate is completely melted and incorporated. Add half of the chopped bacon.

ASSEMBLY Cut the cake into 8 slices and arrange on a plate. Spoon a generous amount of chocolate bacon sauce on the top of each slice, and sprinkle with the remaining bacon bits.

CHOCOLATE TURMERIC CARAMELS

{ MAKES 24 CARAMELS }

Soft and chewy, the lavish measure of butter in this recipe ensures that these luscious, chocolatey caramels melt in your mouth—but don't stick to your teeth. Cooking sugar with a food thermometer can be a bit intimidating; the key is to be sure it is cooking at the right temperature. Take the time to follow each step carefully and don't burn your fingers on hot caramel. Otherwise, this is an easy candy to make for some wonderful holiday treats.

INSTRUCTIONS Line a deep 9 × 9–inch (23 × 23 cm) pan with greased parchment paper, making sure the paper extends ½ inch (1 cm) on each side of the pan.

In a large stainless-steel saucepan, bring the sugar and corn syrup to a boil. Remove from heat and add half of the whipping cream with the chopped chocolate, salt, vanilla extract and turmeric. Whisk until the chocolate has melted and all the ingredients are fully incorporated.

Return saucepan to the stove over medium heat and slowly bring to a boil while stirring with a wooden spoon. Once the mixture begins to boil, add the other half of the whipping cream. Continue boiling until the mixture reaches a temperature of 230°F (110°C). Add the butter and continue boiling while stirring with a wooden spoon until the mixture reaches 240°F (115°C).

Immediately pour the caramel mixture into the prepared pan and let it sit at room temperature for about 4 hours, until cool and hardened.

Lift the caramel out of the pan by lifting the parchment paper. Transfer to a cutting board and gently rub the entire surface of the caramel with some vegetable oil. Cut the caramel into 2-inch (5 cm) squares and wrap each one in a waxed paper or clear cellophane square, twisting both ends to seal the candy. Store in an airtight container in a cool place up to 1 month.

INGREDIENTS

1½ cups (375 mL) granulated sugar

1¼ cups (310 mL) light corn syrup

1¾ cups (430 mL) whipping cream, divided

1 cup (250 mL) chopped extra bitter chocolate

⅛ tsp (0.5 mL) sea salt

½ tsp (2.5 mL) vanilla extract

1 tsp (5 mL) turmeric powder

1 cup (250 mL) cold unsalted butter

¼ cup (60 mL) vegetable oil

Wax paper or cellophane for wrapping

RED VELVET CAKE WITH WHITE CHOCOLATE FROSTING

{ MAKES ONE 9-INCH (23 CM) CAKE }

I'm never sure which part is better to indulge in: the delectable red velvet cake or simply the white chocolate frosting. Maybe both equally? You decide.

RED VELVET CAKE

2½ cups (625 mL) all-purpose flour

1¼ cups (310 mL) granulated sugar

½ tsp (2.5 mL) sea salt

1 tsp (5 mL) baking soda

1 Tbsp (15 mL) cocoa powder

1½ cups (375 mL) canola oil

3 large eggs

1 cup (250 mL) buttermilk

½ tsp (2.5 mL) fresh grated lemon zest

2 Tbsp (30 mL) red food colouring

1 tsp (5 mL) apple cider vinegar

WHITE CHOCOLATE FROSTING

1½ cups (375 mL) chopped white chocolate

¾ cup (180 mL) softened unsalted butter

1 cup (250 mL) icing sugar

¼ tsp (1 mL) sea salt

INSTRUCTIONS FOR RED VELVET CAKE Preheat oven to 350°F (175°C).

In a large bowl, stir together the flour, sugar, salt, baking soda and cocoa powder.

In a medium bowl, whisk together the canola oil and eggs with a hand whisk. Add the buttermilk, lemon zest, food colouring and apple cider vinegar and mix until smooth without creating too many bubbles.

Pour the liquid mixture into the dry and stir with a rubber spatula until the cake batter is smooth.

Grease the inside of a 9-inch (23 cm) nonstick springform pan and dust with flour. Pour the batter into the pan and bake for about 35 minutes, until the sides of the cake pull away from the pan. Once baked, the tip of a knife or a toothpick inserted into the centre of the cake should come out clean.

Remove cake from oven and place on a cooling rack.

INSTRUCTIONS FOR WHITE CHOCOLATE FROSTING Place a double boiler over medium heat. Add the white chocolate to the bowl, and allow it to melt slowly. Keep warm until needed.

In an electric mixing bowl with the whisk attachment, whisk the butter until smooth.

Scrape down the sides of the bowl to ensure there are no lumps.

Pour the melted chocolate over the whipped butter. Mix on medium speed for 1 minute, then add the icing sugar and salt. Continue mixing for 2 minutes until the mixture is light in consistency. Scrape down the sides of the bowl to ensure the frosting is smooth.

ASSEMBLY Cut the cake in half horizontally and position the bottom layer on a serving plate. Spread ¼ inch (0.5 cm) of the frosting on the bottom layer. Place the other layer on top and, using your hand, gently press both layers together. Using a spatula, spread the rest of the frosting over the cake, covering it completely.

CHOCOLATE PECAN BUTTER TART

{ MAKES ONE 9-INCH (23 CM) TART }

What began as a classic butter tart recipe, going back generations, evolved as it was passed around to family and friends. The most recent generation rebelled against using raisins—that's when pecans were substituted in. Then those same raisin rebels became obsessed with adding chocolate to everything. Et voila, the Chocolate Pecan Butter Tart was born. These certainly taste better with homemade almond pate sablée, but frozen store-bought pastry shells work well in a pinch.

ALMOND PATE SABLÉE DOUGH

¾ cup (375 mL) diced cold unsalted butter

½ tsp (2.5 mL) sea salt

2 cups (500 mL) cake flour

1 cup (250 mL) icing sugar

¼ cup (60 mL) ground almonds

1 large egg, beaten

CHOCOLATE PECAN BUTTER FILLING

3 Tbsp (45 mL) softened unsalted butter

1 cup (250 mL) packed golden sugar

1 large egg

1 Tbsp (15 mL) vanilla extract

Pinch of salt

⅓ cup (80 mL) chopped pecans

¼ cup (60 mL) semisweet or bittersweet chocolate chips

INSTRUCTIONS FOR ALMOND PATE SABLÉE DOUGH In an electric mixing bowl with the paddle attachment, add the diced butter, salt and flour and mix on low speed until the mixture resembles small crumbs. Add the icing sugar and ground almonds and mix for 1 minute. Add the beaten egg and continue mixing at low speed until the dough comes together.

Turn the dough out on a lightly floured work surface and finish kneading with your hands. Shape into a ½-inch (1 cm) thick rectangle, wrap in plastic and refrigerate for 1 hour. The dough can be made days ahead.

INSTRUCTIONS FOR CHOCOLATE PECAN BUTTER FILLING Using an electric mixer with the whisk attachment, mix together the butter and sugar at low speed until smooth. Add the egg and vanilla and stir until smooth in texture. Sprinkle in the salt and mix. Stir in the pecans then the chocolate chips.

Place in a container and set aside at room temperature.

ASSEMBLY Preheat oven to 375°F (190°C).

Place the pate sablée dough on a lightly floured work surface and roll until ¼ inch (0.5 cm) thick and about 13 inches (33 cm) in diameter.

Place the dough into a 9-inch (23 cm) tart ring, pressing into the sides to form the edges of the shell. Using a small knife, cut out the excess dough. Place the tart in the refrigerator for 10 minutes.

Remove the tart shell from the fridge and pour in the chocolate pecan filling up to the top. Place in the oven and bake for 7 minutes, then reduce temperature to 350°F (175°C) and bake for another 10 to 12 minutes, until the filling is slightly bubbling and has a light caramel colour.

Transfer tart to a cooling rack. Once cooled, remove the baked tart from the tart ring and place on a serving platter.

ORANGE CHOCOLATE BANANA LOAF

{ MAKES ONE 9.5 × 5-INCH (24 × 13 CM) LOAF }

The key to great-tasting banana bread is ripe—but not overly ripe—bananas. If the bananas are too ripe, the flavour will be bitter. In this recipe, the addition of orange and chocolate deliciously complement the rich banana flavour.

INGREDIENTS

1¾ cups (430 mL) all-purpose flour

1 cup (250 mL) granulated sugar

1 Tbsp (15 mL) baking powder

1 tsp (5 mL) baking soda

2 bananas, mashed

Zest from 1 large orange

⅓ cup (80 mL) vegetable oil

½ cup (125 mL) orange juice

1 tsp (5 mL) vanilla extract

1 large egg, beaten

⅓ cup (80 mL) semisweet chocolate chips

INSTRUCTIONS Preheat oven to 350°F (175°C).

In a medium bowl, combine all the dry ingredients and stir with a whisk.

In an electric mixing bowl with the paddle attachment, mash the bananas on low, then add the orange zest, vegetable oil, orange juice, vanilla extract and beaten egg. Increase speed to medium for a few seconds, then add the dry ingredients and mix on low until everything is just fully incorporated—you don't want to overmix it. Stir in the chocolate chips and try to distribute them evenly in the batter.

Grease a 9.5 × 5-inch (24 × 13 cm) loaf pan by hand and pour the batter in. Bake for 50 minutes for a single loaf pan or 25 minutes for the small pans. Once baked, the tip of a knife or a toothpick inserted into the centre of the cake should come out clean.

Remove loaf or loaves from the oven and let them cool in the pan(s) on a rack. If you remove them too soon from the mould, parts of the loaf bottom could stick to the pan.

DARK CHOCOLATE LEMON TRUFFLES

{ MAKES 24 TRUFFLES }

Lemon and chocolate are not a flavour combination that you often see. This truffle recipe was inspired by my time in Paris, working at the world-renowned La Maison du Chocolat, Rue du Faubourg Saint-Honoré. Every day we would whip up some of the most delicious chocolates, this chocolate lemon truffle among them.

INGREDIENTS

1 vanilla bean

½ cup (125 mL) whipping cream

½ cup (125 mL) whole milk

8 white sugar cubes

2 whole lemons

2¼ cups (560 mL) chopped bittersweet chocolate, divided

2 cups (500 mL) granulated sugar

INSTRUCTIONS Take 1 lemon at a time and grate the skin of the lemon with a sugar cube. The sugar cubes will absorb the oil of the lemon skin as well as the zest.

In a medium saucepan, add the whipping cream and milk. Bring to a boil over medium heat, then remove from heat and whisk in all the sugar cubes. Stir well until the sugar is dissolved.

Place a double boiler over low heat. Add 1¼ cups (310 mL) bittersweet chocolate to the bowl and let it slowly melt. Pour the cream over the melted chocolate and gently stir with a wooden spoon until smooth. Cover with plastic wrap and place in the refrigerator for 4 hours.

Once chilled, use a spoon to scoop and shape the chilled chocolate into balls the size of walnuts. Place the truffles on a tray and let them air dry for 2 hours in a cool setting.

In a medium bowl, add the granulated sugar. Using a small paring knife, cut open the vanilla bean lengthwise and scrape out the seeds into the granulated sugar. Stir the vanilla into the sugar until combined, then spread the sugar evenly on a parchment-lined baking tray. Set aside until needed.

Melt the remaining chocolate in a double boiler, then dip each truffle into the chocolate, coating it completely. Shake off any excess chocolate and roll in the vanilla-infused sugar, then place back on the tray.

Once the chocolate coating has hardened, place the truffles in an airtight container and store in a cool area until ready to serve. Truffles can be kept up to 4 weeks.

"EVERYTHING" CHOCOLATE BROWNIES

{ MAKES ONE 13 × 9-INCH (33 × 23) BAKING TRAY }

The hefty addition of nuts, seeds and dried fruits will add some healthy crunch to these simple yet delicious chocolate brownies, and just a few scrumptious bites will provide helpful calories (that get worked off) when you're hiking or biking. As for me, I enjoy them sitting by a campfire with a cup of coffee.

INGREDIENTS

1¼ cups (310 mL) chopped extra bitter chocolate

4 large eggs

1½ cups (375 mL) granulated sugar

1 cup (250 mL) light brown sugar

2 cups (500 mL) melted unsalted butter

¼ cup (60 mL) chopped walnuts

¼ cup (60 mL) chopped hazelnuts

¼ cup (60 mL) chopped almonds

¼ cups (60 mL) dried cranberries

¼ cups (60 mL) pumpkin seeds

Zest of 1 orange

2 cups (500 mL) all-purpose flour

¼ cup (60 mL) icing sugar

INSTRUCTIONS Preheat oven at 360°F (180°C).

Place a double boiler over medium heat. Add the extra bitter chocolate to the bowl, and allow it to melt slowly. Keep warm until needed.

In an electric mixing bowl with the whisk attachment, whisk the eggs, granulated sugar and brown sugar together on medium speed for 7 minutes. Gently fold in the melted butter and chocolate, then stir until the mixture is smooth.

In a large bowl, stir together the nuts, cranberries, pumpkin seeds, orange zest and flour with a wooden spatula. Using a rubber spatula, fold the flour mixture into the whipped egg mixture.

Fit a 13 × 9-inch (33 × 23) baking tray with parchment paper and spread the batter over the entire area using an offset spatula. Using a small sieve, dust the entire pan with icing sugar.

Bake for 15 minutes, then remove from the oven and place on a cooling rack. Cool for 2 hours, then cut into squares of your preferred size. Store in an airtight container in a cool place up to 2 weeks.

CHOCOLATE TANGERINE SABLÉS

{ MAKES 24 COOKIES }

I love making these rich, buttery, French-style cookies during the holiday season, as they are the perfect homemade gift for friends and work colleagues. The tangerine zest and ground cardamom bring a lot of freshness to the strong chocolate flavour.

INSTRUCTIONS In a medium bowl, stir together the flour, tangerine zest, salt, cocoa powder and cardamom.

In an electric mixing bowl with the paddle attachment, cream the butter and icing sugar on low speed until it just comes together, about 2 minutes. Do not overmix or you risk aerating the dough too much. Add the 2 eggs, one by one, and continue to mix until incorporated. Use a rubber spatula to scrape down the sides of the bowl. Add the flour mixture and mix on low speed for 1 minute.

Turn out the dough onto a lightly floured work surface and finish kneading by hand until all the ingredients are incorporated. The dough will have a beautifully uniform dark-chocolate colour. Shape into a 1½-inch (4 cm) thick rectangular brick and wrap in plastic. Place in the refrigerator for 2 hours.

Preheat oven to 370°F (185°C).

Unwrap the dough and place on a lightly floured work surface. Using a wooden rolling pin, roll out the dough until ½ inch (1 cm) thick, then cut into 2-inch (5 cm) round cookies and place on a parchment-lined baking tray, spacing the cookies 1 inch (2.5 cm) apart from each other.

Brush the top of each cookie with the egg wash and sprinkle with granulated sugar. Bake for 10 minutes, then remove from the oven and place on a cooling rack. Once cooled, transfer the sablés to an airtight container and store in a cool dry place up to 1 month.

INGREDIENTS

2 cups (500 mL) all-purpose flour

Zest of 2 tangerines

½ tsp (2.5 mL) sea salt

¼ cup (60 mL) unsweetened cocoa powder

¼ tsp (1 mL) cardamom

¾ cup (180 mL) softened unsalted butter

1 cup (250 mL) icing sugar

2 large eggs + 1 large egg for egg wash

½ cup (125 mL) granulated sugar

CHOCOLATE LAVA CAKE WITH SWEET AND SALTY PEANUTS

{ MAKES 6 LAVA CAKES }

This cake can be made a day in advance, freeing up time for any other meal preparation. The salted, candied peanuts certainly elevate the taste experience of this classic warm dessert. Once both parts of the recipe are ready, it takes only 7 minutes to bake these delicious chocolatey treats. Top with a scoop of vanilla ice cream and you are in dessert heaven.

CHOCOLATE CAKE BATTER

1 cup (250 mL) chopped extra bitter chocolate

⅔ cup (160 mL) softened unsalted butter + extra for greasing

5 large eggs

⅔ cup (160 mL) granulated sugar

¼ cup (60 mL) all-purpose flour

SWEET AND SALTY PEANUTS

2 cups (500 cups) icing sugar

2 tsp (10 mL) sea salt

1 vanilla bean

1 cup (250 mL) unsalted roasted peanuts (no shells)

Vanilla ice cream for serving

INSTRUCTIONS FOR CHOCOLATE CAKE BATTER In a double boiler over medium heat, melt the chocolate and butter and keep warm until needed.

In an electric mixing bowl with the whisk attachment, beat the eggs and sugar together for 5 minutes until the mixture is fluffy. Using a rubber spatula, gently fold in the chocolate and butter mixture, then fold in the flour. Transfer the batter to a large bowl, cover with plastic wrap and refrigerate for at least 8 hours.

INSTRUCTIONS FOR SWEET AND SALTY PEANUTS Preheat oven to 330°F (160°C).

In a medium bowl, stir together the icing sugar and salt. Slice the vanilla bean lengthwise, scrape out the seeds and combine into the sugar mixture.

In a large saucepan, bring 3 cups (750 mL) water to a boil. Once boiling, remove from heat and add the peanuts. Leave them to sit for 5 minutes, then strain through a fine mesh sieve. Immediately toss the peanuts into the icing sugar bowl then stir until all the peanuts are evenly coated.

Place the peanuts on a parchment-lined baking tray and bake until they start to caramelize into a light golden colour, about 10 minutes. Remove from the oven and break apart the clusters of peanuts using a spatula. Place on a rack to cool for about 1 hour.

ASSEMBLY Increase oven temperature to 370°F (185°C).

Grease the insides of the six 1-cup (250 mL) ramequins with vegetable oil or butter. Place the ramequins on a baking tray evenly spaced.

Fit a piping bag with a large round tip. Using a rubber spatula, fill the piping bag with the chocolate cake batter and pipe into the ramequins until each is three-quarters full.

Bake for 8 minutes, then remove from the oven and place on a cooling rack for 5 minutes. Using a hand towel, place the ramequins on 6 small plates. Sprinkle with a generous amount of the peanuts and finish with a scoop of vanilla ice cream.

IRRESISTIBLE CHOCOLATE HAZELNUT COOKIES

{ MAKES 36 COOKIES }

Joachim Splichal, the chef behind renowned Los Angeles restaurant Patina, gave me this recipe on my first day on the job there as Pastry Chef. "They are irresistible," were his words. And indeed, these cookies are irresistible and delicious.

INSTRUCTIONS In an electric mixing bowl with the paddle attachment, cream together the butter and sugar on low speed. Use a rubber spatula to scrape down the sides of the bowl. Continue mixing on low speed, then add the yolks one at a time until fully incorporated.

Place a double boiler over medium heat. Add the bittersweet chocolate to the bowl, and allow it to melt slowly.

Add the melted chocolate, ground hazelnuts and flour to the butter mixture and mix on low speed until the dough just comes together. It's important not to overmix the dough, which will feel a bit soft at first but will firm once the melted chocolate starts to solidify. Wrap in plastic and refrigerate for 30 minutes.

Preheat oven to 360°F (180°C).

Remove the dough from the fridge and, using a soup spoon, shape it into balls the size of egg yolks. Place the dough balls on a parchment-lined baking tray, spacing each ball 2 inches (5 cm) apart from each other. Dust the tops of the cookies with icing sugar and bake for 12 minutes.

Remove from the oven and let them cool completely on a rack. Store in an airtight container in a dry place up to 1 month.

INGREDIENTS

1 cup (250 mL) softened unsalted butter

1 cup (250 mL) granulated sugar

3 large egg yolks

1 cup (50 mL) chopped extra bitter chocolate

1½ cups (375 mL) ground hazelnuts

½ cup (125 mL) all-purpose flour

½ cup (125 mL) icing sugar

CHOCOLATE AND BANANA TOASTER PASTRIES

{ MAKES 12 PASTRIES }

There is no better way to reconnect with your inner child than spending time in the kitchen making toaster pastries (i.e., Pop-Tarts) and recreating memories. It is better to prepare the banana filling the day before.

BANANA FILLING

1 cup (250 mL) chopped white chocolate

¼ cup (60 mL) light brown sugar

3 Tbsp (45 mL) cornstarch

1 cup (250 mL) whole milk

3 ripe bananas, peeled and diced to ¼-inch (0.5 cm) cubes with a chef's knife

¼ cup (60 mL) softened unsalted butter

PASTRY DOUGH

2½ cups (625 mL) all-purpose flour

¼ cup (60 mL) unsweetened cocoa powder

2 Tbsp (30 mL) granulated sugar

¼ tsp (1 mL) sea salt

¼ tsp (1 mL) ground cinnamon

¼ tsp (1 mL) baking powder

1 cup (250 mL) diced cold unsalted butter

½ cup (125 mL) whole milk

1 large egg for egg wash

INSTRUCTIONS FOR BANANA FILLING In a double boiler over medium heat, melt the chocolate and keep warm until needed.

In a small bowl, mix together the sugar and cornstarch.

In a medium saucepan, bring the milk to a boil over medium heat. Remove from heat and stir in the sugar mixture along with the diced bananas. Return saucepan to the stove and bring to a quick boil while stirring. Remove from heat and whisk in the melted chocolate and butter.

Pour the filling into a small container and cover the top with plastic wrap touching the surface to avoid steam. Chill in the refrigerator before using.

INSTRUCTIONS FOR PASTRY DOUGH In an electric mixer with the paddle attachment, combine the flour, cocoa powder, sugar, salt, cinnamon and baking powder on low speed for 30 seconds, then add the butter and milk. Keep mixing at low speed until the dough comes together. (It might be necessary to add an extra 1 to 2 Tbsp/15 to 30 mL of milk if the dough feels too dry.)

Turn the dough out on to a lightly floured work surface and knead the dough by hand until smooth. Wrap in plastic and place in the refrigerator for 15 minutes.

Once the dough is chilled, place on a lightly floured surface and use a wooden rolling pin to roll it out ⅛ inch (3 mm) thick. Cut the dough into twelve 4 × 3-inch (10 × 8 cm) rectangles. Place the rectangles on a parchment-lined baking tray and place in the refrigerator to chill for 30 minutes.

INSTRUCTIONS FOR CHOCOLATE GLAZE In a medium saucepan, bring the condensed milk, vanilla extract and whole milk to a boil over medium heat. Remove from heat and whisk in the chocolate, icing sugar and cocoa powder. Pour through a fine mesh sieve. Set aside at room temperature until needed.

ASSEMBLY Place 1 Tbsp (15 mL) chilled banana filling on half of the dough rectangles, leaving each with a ¼-inch (0.5 cm) border. Brush the edges of each tart with beaten egg, then lay the other half of the dough over the filling and seal the edges by pinching with the back of a fork. Brush the top of each tart with more egg wash. Place the ready-to-bake tarts in the fridge for 30 minutes to chill.

Heat oven to 370°F (185°C). Once chilled, place the tarts in the oven and bake for 15 minutes.

Remove tarts from the oven and place on a cooling rack. After 10 minutes, spoon a layer of chocolate glaze on the top of each tart. Let it set for 1 hour at room temperature.

Store tarts in an airtight container up to 2 days, if you can keep these delicious treats from being eaten that long.

CHOCOLATE GLAZE

1 cup (250 mL) condensed milk

1 tsp (5 mL) vanilla extract

½ cup (125 mL) whole milk

¼ cup (60 mL) chopped semi-sweet chocolate

2 cups (500 mL) icing sugar

¼ cup (60 mL) unsweetened cocoa powder

CHOCOLATE MERINGUE KISSES

{ MAKES 24 KISSES }

Meringues are cloud-like delectable treats that are oh-so-light that they seem like they could be calorie free. Not! But they are perfect to give (and receive), especially for those with a gluten intolerance.

INGREDIENTS

½ cup (125 mL) chopped dark chocolate

½ cup (125 mL) icing sugar

1 Tbsp (15 mL) cornstarch

3 Tbsp (45 mL) unsweetened cocoa powder

½ cup (125 mL) egg whites

½ cup (125 mL) granulated sugar

INSTRUCTIONS Preheat oven to 240°F (115°C).

Place a double boiler over medium heat. Add the bittersweet chocolate to the bowl, and allow it to melt slowly. Keep warm until needed.

In a medium bowl, mix together the icing sugar, cornstarch and cocoa powder.

In an electric mixing bowl with the whisk attachment, whip the egg whites on medium speed. Once the egg whites start to foam and increase in volume by a third, increase to high speed and gradually incorporate the granulated sugar. Whip until soft peaks form.

Remove bowl from the mixer and gently fold in the icing sugar mixture with a rubber spatula. Try to avoid deflating the whipped egg whites in the process.

Spoon the whipped egg whites into a piping bag fitted with a star tip. Pipe 2-inch (5 cm) rounds of meringue onto a parchment-lined baking tray, spacing the rounds 1 inch (2.5 cm) apart from each other.

Bake for 2 hours, until the meringue kisses are dry and crispy. Remove from the oven and place on a cooling rack.

Once the meringue kisses have cooled, use a fork to drizzle melted chocolate over the tops. Let the kisses set for 1 hour then store in an airtight container in a cool dry place up to 1 month.

IT TAKES A VILLAGE

A heartfelt thank you to the entire team behind this amazing cookbook project. Love and gratitude for your help, talent and support.

My son Sergio For being my light and heartbeat and my best partner on the ski hills!

Arata Arai Thanks for the lovely illustration found at the beginning of the book.

Holly and Sharon Fitzhenry, Fitzhenry & Whiteside Thank you for your trust and support in developing my first cookbook and making my second cookbook a dream come true.

Henry Wu A trendsetter foodie who over the course of 25 years reshaped the Toronto food scene. When no one knew what yuzu or ponzu was, we were already serving it. Over the years you've been a boss, investor, friend and, for our second photographic project together, an amazing photographer with a keen eye.

Rossy Earle and Miriam Echeverria The magic team, masters of creations. Thank you for testing recipes and making the food look amazing in the photographs.

Andrei Godoroja For taking the time to test many of the recipes in the book, resulting in valuable feedback.

Anastasia Galadza and Mark Kneeshaw For your talents as photography assistants, organizers and master planners.

The Food Group Studio, Toronto A remarkable, inspiring and creative space in the heart of Toronto. A dream stage for any photographer with a huge "prop-alooza" room. It made our photo shoot go so smoothly.

Whitecap Books From design to sales and marketing, a big thank you for making this book a success.

BAKING
WITH
BRUNO
LOVE STORY
PHOTOGRAPHY BY
Henry M. Wu
Bruno Feldeisen
Henry M. Wu

INDEX

MASTERS OF
FOOD & WINE
HIGHLANDS INN
Bruno Feldeisen

HOBART
Arctic

T

V

W

Y